SUSAN A. JENNINGS

Save Some for Me

And how about you?

First published by Susan Jennings 2019

Copyright © 2019 by Susan A. Jennings

All rights reserved. No part of this publication may be reproduced, stored or transmitted in any form or by any means, electronic, mechanical, photocopying, recording, scanning, or otherwise without written permission from the publisher. It is illegal to copy this book, post it to a website, or distribute it by any other means without permission.

Susan A. Jennings asserts the moral right to be identified as the author of this work.

Susan A. Jennings has no responsibility for the persistence or accuracy of URLs for external or third-party Internet Websites referred to in this publication and does not guarantee that any content on such Websites is, or will remain, accurate or appropriate.

Designations used by companies to distinguish their products are often claimed as trademarks. All brand names and product names used in this book and on its cover are trade names, service marks, trademarks and registered trademarks of their respective owners. The publishers and the book are not associated with any product or vendor mentioned in this book. None of the companies referenced within the book have endorsed the book.

Author photographs by Doris Leightley

Cover design by Rebecca Covers

Cover image: Voyages to Inner Paint/@agsandrew/Depositphotos

Second edition

ISBN: 978-1-989553-03-9

This book was professionally typeset on Reedsy.
Find out more at reedsy.com

This book is dedicated to
My five amazing children
Their children, nine awesome grandchildren
My incredibly strong mother and understanding father
Without their adventurous spirit and support
I would not be who I am today

"We all get where we're going by circuitous journeys, and some of the setbacks are warranted."

Carol Burnett

Contents

Author's Note - Now and Before

Save Some for Me is the true story of a large part of my life. Initially, I felt it necessary to protect the privacy of my family and friends by changing names of people and places. In this edition, I continued with fake personal names but the places are real. The book was written as I perceived and remembered the world at that time and as it related to my family and our daily lives.

The story is about my expectations as a young bride, the wonderful things that I enjoyed as a wife and mother, that so quickly turned into a fearful and unpleasant life. It ended in heartbreak and disillusionment, followed by years of raising five children alone. I want to pass on to other women some strategies and methods I used to keep going. Most of them are simple, many of them I just did at the time without really knowing the outcome, but following my inner prompting. There is a lot to be said for the 'mother bear' instinct.

I've noticed that people today need to validate good advice as coming from a qualified source, a book or therapist. I beg to differ. Who is more qualified, the mother who gave birth to her children or a complete stranger? Although I learned a great deal from books and therapy, it was my 'mother bear' instinct that guided me through most of the hard times.

My message is simple: be true to yourself and trust your instincts. You will make it through, and there is a good life waiting for you after the children are grown. You will find enough energy to enjoy many years and experience life on your own terms, not at the whim of others.

I took the next paragraph directly from the introduction of the first edition…

"Hello, I call to a friend," as she approaches. "How are you?" Being polite I reply, with a smile, "I'm fine, just peachy!" Such a silly expression! How can you be peachy unless you are a piece of fruit? Mind you, it is just as silly as saying I am fine, because if the truth were known I am not fine. I am 59 years old, give or take a year or two, my bones ache, my blonde hair comes out of a Clairol bottle to cover the grey and I am 50 plus pounds overweight. I have no job to speak of and I am just about at the end of my savings that were supposed to be for my retirement. The kids are long gone. It's just little old me and my 17-year-old dog, Trixie.

Now fast forward eighteen years…

The greeting and reply might be similar, although I doubt I'd use peachy, but I would say I was fine and honestly, right now, I am fine. I am 78 years old. My bones ache even more. My bottled blond hair is naturally grey and I've added a few purple, pink and blue streaks. I am still 50 pounds overweight. I do have a job, although not the 9-5 kind, and I love it. I'm a novelist and 'authorpreneur.' That pays pennies per book, so I'm still broke. My savings are completely gone. I am not retired, by choice, nor will I ever retire. My kids are long gone and now my grandkids are grown up. It is still little old me and a dog; Miss Penny is a two-year-old Shih Tzu and I am, surprisingly happy and as close to my authentic self as anyone can get.

Back to 2003. I wrote this book for women who are divorced single mothers, or single mothers with no father in the picture, who have raised kids under incredibly difficult circumstances. A tornado just went through your life sucking you up into a funnel and then scattering little pieces of you everywhere. I stood in the ruins, battered and bruised, licking my wounds and looking around with an uneasy calm. I wasn't afraid of the storm, but I had no idea how to put my life together.

There are many stories similar to mine, some worse, some not so bad, but all are heart wrenching accounts of brave and courageous women who sacrificed much in their lives to raise families on their own. Many feel physically, emotionally and financially drained. By sharing my story, I hope to inspire all women who have raised children under difficult circumstances to know that they are not alone.

Once I learned to reach out, I found great comfort knowing that I was not alone. I drew strength from female friends as we laughed and cried together. I discovered how to pick up the pieces and become whole again. *Save Some for Me* will help you find the calm after the storm, to relax and enjoy the next 25 or so years of your life.

The stories describe events, situations and outcomes, as well as possible scenarios and lessons learned. Although the kids are gone and life has changed, many of the habits and gut reactions linger on, causing problems. Some women become martyrs, some develop clinical depression. Others have become chirpy, smiley types, covering the pain, while raging inside. Many are angry, grouchy and just plain miserable to be with. I know I can plead guilty to all of these symptoms at one time or another.

Whoever said life was fair?

Save Some for Me helps women to get over it, to identify and acknowledge any crippling behaviour, to build on strengths, embrace the things in life that give pleasure, enjoy retirement and the rest of life. We deserve it. Come join me in reclaiming a joyful life as we learn how to: *Save Some for Me! And what about you?*

1

That Fateful Day My Marriage Ended

The old grandfather clock struck five as Rodney opened the front door earlier than usual. The children were in the family room watching TV and I was in the kitchen preparing supper. There was no greeting, only the suggestion he pour me a gin and tonic. "No thanks," I said with a frown. It was Tuesday and I don't drink mid-week as a rule.

Rodney insisted. "I'll make it a double, you are going to need it."

I was not a big drinker but Rodney was and like most drunks, he liked company when he drank so I naively thought we were in for another session with the booze. But something was different. His attitude was kind and gentle and he seemed quite nervous. I didn't hear his usual sarcastic or abusive tone, which warned me that I was in for a rough night. There was something about the way he asked me to sit down, the concern in his voice that told me this was serious. Anxiety gripped my insides. Something was very wrong. I accepted the gin and tonic, lit a cigarette, inhaled deeply and braced myself.

I was not prepared for what happened next. I have never had an out-of-body experience, but that is what it felt like. This couldn't be happening to me. Rodney's words seemed hollow and far away.

"I'm leaving you. I have found someone else." He paused and added, "I can't stand the kids, this house or Blackburn Hamlet." And that was it! One sentence of the most hurtful words I have ever heard either before or since that fateful day.

I just sat there at the kitchen table, unable to speak. Stunned, I didn't even cry. *It's a nightmare. I will wake up in a minute. This is a mistake,* I thought. *I must have misheard what he said. He didn't mean to say those things. He'll apologize. He's been drinking.*But I knew he hadn't. I was in denial. Deep down I knew that my life had changed forever, nothing would ever be the same again and I had never felt so alone in my entire life.

My first thought was for the children. I had to keep it together for them. They had no idea what Mom and Dad were talking about, although I am sure you could have cut the atmosphere with a knife. But then again, that was not unusual. I had to keep going. The gin and tonic was a good idea. Surprisingly, it helped me stay focused.

Something was strangling my whole body; my throat, so tight I could hardly breathe, as I fought back tears. My head was spinning so fast that I couldn't see. My heart pounded in my ears and throbbed in my chest. Way in the distance I heard Nathan, our eldest son ask, "when will supper be ready, Mom?" His voice jolted me back but I couldn't speak. I got up from the kitchen table and like a robot, I served supper.

The meal was a somber occasion and even the kids were quiet, sensing something was not right, but not daring to say anything. The rest of the evening seemed normal. I did my usual chores—clearing away the supper dishes and tidying the kitchen, while the older kids, Nathan 14, Katrina 12 and William 10 did their homework without any fuss for once.

I went upstairs to bathe the babies as we fondly called Alex and James, although they were now four and five years old. Their closeness in age meant that we often treated them as twins. The four years between William and Alex made it appear that we had two families, thus emphasizing the smallness of the "little ones."

My stomach was in knots and my hands trembled, but I kept smiling, talking and playing with the kids as though nothing had happened. What a struggle to keep my voice controlled. I got everyone to bed early. I needed some time to myself to think. I felt strange, as though I was outside my body on autopilot. Everything seemed so far away and time stood still. I was trying to figure out what had happened and what was going to happen but at the same time I didn't want to think about it.

Rodney had gone out, under some pretense of having to meet a student. A family physician and professor at Ottawa University, he was part of a team that trained medical students in the art of family medicine. The student excuse had been used often. I just hadn't realized it was an excuse. I thought he was a dedicated teacher. He reassured me that he wouldn't be long, again with this gentle concern in his voice, as if he really cared. I guessed he was going to report the evening's announcement to the girlfriend. I am not sure what he thought I might do, but obviously it was not bad enough to make him stay home.

I sat in the living room, staring at the wall and the furniture we had spent years saving to buy. How could I make sense of what had happened? The questions started swirling around my head. Why? Why would he do this? Why did I not see it coming? What did I do wrong? The questions were endless; I began to go over the events of the last six months. What were the warning signs? What had I missed? How could I solve the problem?

Although our marriage had been troubled for some time, I naively thought that things would eventually just work out. Family life was stressful and the children took up most of my time. Rodney worked long hours, so we didn't have a lot of time for each other. I thought it was just the way things had to be when you had a large active family. As the children grew older and Rodney's career was established, I expected that Rodney and I would find more time and we would grow together again. In fact, I thought it was already happening. The last six months had been relatively happy. The drinking had almost stopped. He was in fairly good humour most of the time and the abusive behaviour and sarcasm had lessened.

However, I sensed that something was wrong. I remember confiding in my friend who lived next door. "Joan, I am really concerned that he is about to start a drinking binge."

Joan's question caught me off guard. "Are you sure he doesn't have a girlfriend?"

"Girlfriend?" I said without hesitation. "I don't think so." Trying to be realistic, I replied, "of course it is a possibility, but I don't think so, not Rodney."

The memory of his relationship with Isabel flashed in my mind. She had died of cancer two years earlier. Was I naïve enough to think it couldn't happen again? Isabel, a nurse practitioner at a St. John's Clinic, had worked closely with Rodney setting it up. A worthy cause, it provided much needed medical services for the poorer members of the community who either couldn't or wouldn't go to a doctor for medical help. The clinic was successful but success meant long hours for Rodney as he was now doing two demanding jobs. I remember being proud of Rodney's dedication. I didn't mind the long hours that took him away from us. His family and his patients needed him and he was so happy in his work.

There were a few telltale signs, some quite blatant that the relationship was more than work, but I chose to ignore them. It was unreasonable to work until two or three o'clock in the morning, even at a busy clinic, but I rationalized those long hours. Then there was the weekend work. He was always on call and always with Isabel. I became suspicious, but I simply did not want to know. I had always teased Rodney by saying, "if you ever have an affair, never tell me or let me find out about it." Even in the early years, my way of dealing with my suspicions was denial.

Isabel had a large house with a big backyard and in-ground swimming pool (this was before we had our own pool). The whole family was invited for summer swims. What a farce that was, the three adults pretended this was a normal social gathering. I was in denial. Rodney was perpetuating my denial by trying to convince me that they were just friends and colleagues. A façade that was quite unnecessary as my denial was so deep I saw nothing anyway. The children innocently enjoyed the water and had lots of fun. We would thank Isabel for her hospitality and leave for home. On one occasion Isabel invited just Rodney and I for dinner without the children. Dinner lasted forever. Conversation was stilted at best as I observed Rodney and Isabel exchange loving glances across the table. The objective of the evening was to prove to me that the late nights at the clinic were justified because Isabel liked to talk and I could see how difficult it was to get away. I bought it! I bought the whole story. Can you believe that? Queen of denial!

I finally came to my senses at the Clinic's Christmas Party. I was six months pregnant with James, our fifth child, so I was quiet and sober. Rodney was busy partying and drinking, paying a lot of attention to Isabel and ignoring me. The attention was obvious and even I, queen of denial, could no longer ignore the flirting. The final straw came when Rodney announced to me and the rest of the room that he would be back in a minute; he was walking Isabel to her car. Hand in hand they walked out and as they closed the front door every head in the room turned and looked at me with pity in their eyes. Everyone in the room knew, and had known for a long time, what was going on. Humiliation, barely describes how I felt. I wanted the floor to swallow me up, to scream or cry or run away. But the polite young woman I had been raised to be, carried on as though nothing had happened.

I confronted Rodney when we arrived home. He denied everything and accused me of being paranoid and over sensitive. Hormones had caused my imagination to run away with me.

"Of course there was no affair," he scoffed, flattered that I was jealous. He smiled with this innocent, little boy smile that just melted my anger and I believed him, because that is what I wanted to believe.

Isabel became very sick with cancer shortly after and when she died, it devastated Rodney. He tried to hide it, but how do you hide your feelings when someone close to you dies? His reaction was too intense for someone who was just a co-worker. I couldn't be sympathetic. I was gloating. I felt guilty about gloating, but in my usual passive aggressive way, I wanted him to suffer. He was upset that I had no compassion for him. This was out of character for me as I am naturally compassionate, which made it difficult for him to understand. I did not care.

2

Queen of Denial

I can only imagine how difficult it would be to grieve without showing grief. Rodney's grief and pain first presented itself as anger, even rage. He did eventually talk about it but only after tearing me apart with his anger. Defending myself, an argument ensued and finally he admitted that he had been in love with her and had had an affair. But right now he needed me and, conveniently, he still loved me. As angry as I was, I made excuses for his behaviour, telling myself it was just a fling. Men did these things. They couldn't help themselves. Isabel was no longer a threat and our life would return to normal.

Queen of denial put on her crown again, which was getting heavy as it grew in size. Even as I write this, I am saying to myself, "how could I have been so stupid?" I know that some of you are shaking your heads in disbelief and others are nodding with, *I understand. Been there, done that!*

The Isabel affair had happened five years ago and I assumed it was a one-off, believing it would never happen again. Well, Joan was right. I had missed it again. There was another woman.

Still in the living room, I moved to the big bay window and stared, first up the sleeping street and then in the other direction, nothing stirring to break the silence. It was early morning, still dark, with only a few porch lights pooled brightly on driveways. Dawn would break soon and Rodney was not home. I was in so much pain from the tightness in my stomach and chest and a hole in my broken heart. I was exhausted and, realizing that nothing would take the pain away, I went to bed. I probably wouldn't sleep, but I could let go, cry and scream into my pillow and perhaps the tears of anguish, hurt, betrayal and regret would fade. I eventually fell into a restless sleep.

To my surprise, Rodney came home that night. I pretended not to hear him. I didn't want to talk, to hear more lies, to feel more pain. He crawled into our bed but I stayed on my side, feigning sleep. I thought how crazy it was. There we were, sleeping in the same bed when he had told me before dinner that he couldn't stand me, and surely had just returned from making love with his girlfriend. I look back in disbelief that I allowed him to sleep in my bed, at my side, for two months until he finally moved out.

Day to day living went on as though nothing had happened. I took care of the kids, chatted on the phone, popped in to drink coffee with the neighbours, played bridge on Tuesday nights and never said a word to anyone. From the outside, my life seemed normal. On the inside, I was screaming, the pain unbearable and yet I could not reach out. Why did I choose to suffer in silence? What made me suffer so silently? Saying I wasn't very rational at the time is perhaps an understatement. Was it disbelief? These things happened to other people, not me. To people I don't know, who lived in a different world. It couldn't happen, not to me. The loneliness was so overwhelming that it never occurred to me that other women were going through the same kind of anguish.

Believing that I was the only person who had ever experienced this trauma, I was convinced that no one would understand how I felt. How could they relate to such intense emotional pain? Who would want to listen to my problems and fears? Even thinking about confiding in anyone engulfed me in shame. How could I have allowed this to happen? I was to blame. I wasn't a good enough wife. I didn't look after the children properly. I should have entertained more. I should have been more generous with my time. I should have initiated more sex and I should have been more understanding. So what if he had a few drinks too many? It was no wonder he looked to other women. I wasn't good enough. I was too fat, not pretty enough and it was entirely my fault. I was taking all the blame and feeling the shame of a broken marriage.

I had married for better or worse, so the shame was almost as bad as the hurt. I was too paralyzed to do anything, especially to reach out for help and comfort. What would people say? I was silent on the outside, screaming on the inside. I worked hard at keeping my composure and even my closest friends had no idea that my world had just fallen apart. I knew that I would have to tell someone, sometime. And then there were my parents. How could I tell them?

Two weeks after that fateful day, I plucked up the courage to call a friend. Carol and I were not especially close at the time, but she has become a special friend since. Carol had just gone through a separation so I figured she would understand my situation. She most certainly did. I felt as though a 1000 pound weight had been lifted off my shoulders. It felt so good to be able to confide in someone. Finally able to vent my anger, I talked on and on. Carol's kind ear and comforting words helped ease the pain. Her practical advice, especially on legal matters, was invaluable. Knowing that I was not alone, I was to discover that what I was experiencing was quite normal under the circumstances. I now felt able to call my parents and, gradually, I was able to talk more openly. I so desperately needed the strength of friends and family.

Rodney hadn't told me much about the girlfriend, except he had met her on a French course he attended in the spring, and that it would be a long distance relationship as she was off to Africa in the New Year. It struck me as odd. Why would he be giving up his family for someone who was about to leave the country? It explained why he was in no hurry to move out. I began to think that the girlfriend was not so serious. It even occurred to me that he might change his mind. Could I take him back? This was a loaded question but I didn't have to respond. Rodney answered it for me.

One Sunday afternoon in mid-December I noticed that Rodney was on edge every time the phone rang and he rushed to answer it. This was very unusual for him as he never answered the phone. I put two and two together and realized 'she' must be calling. I was right. The call came and there he was, in our kitchen, within earshot of the children and me, talking to his girlfriend in London, England. She was en route to Africa.

I did something I have never done before or since. I went upstairs, picked up the extension and listened in on the call. The most difficult ten minutes of my life followed.

Perched on the edge of the bed with my hand over the mouthpiece, I tried not to move or breathe. In different circumstances, this picture could be quite funny. The words I heard were heartbreaking. They declared their undying love and lamented how they would miss each other and be miserable while apart. It was sickening. Then she thanked him for the flowers, one dozen red roses for her birthday. One dozen red roses! I was furious. In 16 years of marriage, plus four years of dating, I had never received roses for my birthday or any other occasion.

It was a mistake to listen in. My mother always said that no good came from eavesdropping and she was right. I had heard what I didn't want to hear. This affair was serious and it wasn't going to go away. I had to accept it and figure out how to go on.

It was not the right time to make life-changing decisions, although there was an overwhelming desire to push away the hurt and tears, forget, and move on. I would ultimately do that, but so much pain, anger, grief and disbelief monopolized my thoughts that clear, rational thinking was just impossible. I recognized this at some unconscious level but only remember the fog. Sounds were dulled and images floated by as I functioned on automatic pilot. My mind was reliving and examining events and feelings of the past 20 years. It was like replaying a movie, forward, reverse, pause, then forward again. The movie was our life. Rodney's smile of love, wonder and pride as he held Nathan, our first-born child, or the way he would stroke my long brown hair as he held me close. How he comforted me when I miscarried our second baby. In contrast to these loving acts, there was the sudden unexplained and frightening mood swings. The moods would start by being overly happy, often laughing a forced loud laugh and then suddenly, without warning, he would become angry and lash out in a rage, cursing, complaining and shouting. Then, the silence.

As I recalled these mood swings, my mother's words came to mind "Sticks and stones can break your bones but words will never hurt you." How untrue! Harsh, hurtful words leave deep scars and can have a much more lasting effect than physical hurt and it is much easier for the abuser to hide the behaviour. The abusive words would roll off his tongue as he sat in the living room at nine o'clock in the morning, drinking beer with a gallon of home brew at his feet.

I was completely buried in feelings of betrayal and grief. It was the loss of my husband and the life I had expected; believing without question that my role was to be a wife and mother in a traditional family.

3

Fairy Tales My Mother Told Me

In England in the 1940s, during the Second World War, I was born into an abnormal wartime family lifestyle, although not abnormal by today's standards. Women, who would normally be home taking care of the family, were working in the factories to help fight the war. Men fought the war on battlefields, miles from home. In the absence of males, women took on the role of head of the household. Some men didn't come home, leaving behind widows and orphans. It is surprising to me that life seemed to go back to 'normal.' Widows remarried, women went back into the homes as housewives, and men were once again at the head of the household.

Roles were clearly defined, as they were when my mother was born in 1920. It was as though nothing had happened. The traditional roles and lifestyle survived. In spite of the war, I, like most women of my generation, was raised with pre-war traditions.

As a small child, my play was typically with dolls and houses. Christmas and birthday gifts were dolls, clothes, baby carriages, tea sets, mini baking tins, etc. It seemed they could reproduce all household items in miniature, providing little girls with toys that taught them the finer art of housewifery. My toy box was full of them. I spent hours playing house with other girls. I was being groomed to be a wife and mother. My mother was a very good role model. She taught me to cook, sew, keep house and be a good companion to a husband. I believed that if I was good, kind and did everything right, I would live happily ever after. These expectations were reasonable at that time. In my mind, as a child and teenager, my expectations were fairy tales that would come true.

The biggest fairy tale of them all was my interpretation of being a good girl. Be slim and pretty, be nice, don't argue or talk too much, and your reward will be Prince Charming, tall, dark and handsome, kind, and generous with piles of money. He will sweep you off your feet and carry you off on a galloping white horse, take you to his castle where he will pamper you and take care of you until your dying day. You will have beautiful children and live happily ever after.

What hogwash! No generation has ever lived like that. You only find that in a particularly sickening Disney movie. However, there are some parallels that could be drawn from the fairy tale. Taking care meant that the prince would provide a home, food and clothing. The princess (wife) was a housewife who raised the children and looked after the house. These roles were well defined and everyone had their place and knew what was expected of them. I am sure there were problems, but as a child I did not see them. This was the fairy tale I expected would be my way of life when I grew up.

My father, breadwinner and head of the household, expected his supper on the table when he came home from work. My mother broke from tradition in that she worked outside the home. She had her own hairdressing business and we had a live-in nanny until ill health prompted my mother to sell the business. After my mother regained her health, she worked part time in market research. Instead of having one job, she now had two, as they expected her to ensure the other job did not interfere with the housework and the family needs. When I asked her about this, she responded that her money was for the extras, holidays and luxury items, but daddy was the breadwinner and the boss. Mother's contribution was not valued in the same way. These earnings were never interpreted as essential and often viewed as something to keep the little lady amused. It certainly would not go over well today.

My mother saw the value of having some independence, including her own bank account. This was commendable but only worked if you had some money to put into it. Nevertheless, in the 1950s most women did not have their own bank accounts and although my father tolerated it, many men did not.

Both my parents encouraged me to pursue postsecondary education and I was sent off to college for two years to study Home Economics—another fairy tale, an extension of playing house. The rationale was that I would have something to fall back on if I didn't get married or, heaven forbid, became a widow. The idea was well meant and was quite forward looking for the times. The number of young women attending universities and colleges was small compared to today. I considered it to be a privileged and enjoyed the college experience. I have no doubt that it helped prepare me for the adult world. However, when I became a single parent, not through dreaded widowhood, but worse, divorce, my training was inadequate when I needed work.

When I finished college and entered the workforce my parents looked toward their planned retirement. Since I was no longer a drain on either their finances or time, they now had the resources. I watched them grow closer together and saw in them a passion for each other that I had never seen before. They enjoyed travelling, entertaining and a variety of activities. They laughed a lot and showed a caring for one another that was beautiful to watch. Yet another fairy tale for me as I expected nothing less. But we never made it that far.

My father died of cancer 12 years after he retired, so those years were very precious and my mother cherishes the memories. She still misses him terribly, but was able to assert her independence and keep going. Unlike many widows, she had her own bank account and knew how to run a household. She picked up the pieces and made a new life for herself, made easier by Dad's pension and savings, as well as the inheritance from parents. It was not a large fortune but adequate.

My mother's love of life, appreciation of the world, and desire to learn new things kept her going. Mom turned 83 years young the year this book was published. She still travelled, entertained, and enjoyed cooking for elaborate dinner parties. She continued to drive a car as though she was entering the Indy 500. Fortunately, her mind and reflexes were sharp. If anyone got in her way, it was of course 'their' fault. Beautifully tailored clothes in modern patterns and fabrics, along with high-heeled shoes adorned her slim, toned body. Mother had always taken good care of herself and she had a wonderful attitude towards life. To her, retirement was just another exciting phase of life, one to be embraced and enjoyed.

My retirement years will be nothing like my parents' and I am very envious of anyone who has achieved it. I feel cheated. Cheated out of an inheritance, not only of money or property, but of lifestyle. At this stage of life, I had hoped to be reaping the rewards of a busy and productive life, to have companionship and to be doing the things that I always wanted to do but never had the time. I hope I don't sound like one of those miserable grouchy types, or someone suffering from 'poor me' syndrome. Perhaps I am a little of both, but then whoever said life was fair? Fair or not, the traditional retirement years are what I was expecting and I feel cheated. It is not surprising for any of us raised during that time to expect any less.

The perception of the fairy tale life—happily ever after—was not a deliberate lie. Society changed in the '70s and '80s. The divorce rate climbed, mothers raised children alone, lived with men without marriage and even giving birth out of wedlock was accepted. As a result, the family unit was never the same. These events turned my expectations into truly 'make believe fairy tales,' with no possibility of meeting those childhood expectations. Although divorced single mothers were accepted in some, but few, social circles in the 70s and 80s there were no mentors or guidance for women like me. It was virgin territory with no idea what was ahead, how to prepare or cope. Pioneers, women like myself, struggled with no tools. We learned by our numerous mistakes. The laws pertaining to family and divorce were archaic and no support systems were available.

Friends shunned me because they didn't know how to deal with my circumstances. Was I a threat to their comfortable lives, even a temptation to faithful husbands? "Who was this strange person?"

I wanted to yell out loud. "This strange person was once your friend. The only thing different is that her husband walked out on her and the family. She is now lonely, unhappy and in need of compassion and friendship."

I remember being surprised that so few people stuck by me. Iwas shocked to realize that some men considered the loss of my husband made me easy prey for their advances. Even my female friends ostracized me instead of supporting me in my time of need. I felt like a square peg in a round hole, not fitting in anywhere.

As I reflect on what my expectations had been, the life I had been living, and what it became, it is hard to imagine living in two such different worlds. I had been close to living my fairy tale dream of happily ever after!

4

The Dream That Almost Came True

Tricycles, bicycles, hockey sticks, Barbie dolls, Tonka trucks, toy cars, soccer balls and baseball bats littered the driveway and front lawn. This was a house bustling with five children, two cocker spaniels and three cats (could be more depending on whether or not we had a new litter). One of my friends teasingly referred to me as the lady with ten kids. Her comments always raised a few eyebrows and made me chuckle over a stranger's surprise.

Ten was not far from the truth as my kids always had a bunch of friends over, either in the basement in winter, or the pool in summer. I preferred it that way and enjoyed having the kids around. That way I could keep a casual eye on activities and enjoy the fun. When things got out of hand, I could reprimand or let it slide—picking my battles, but winning the war. I was a stay-at-home mom so I had the luxury of always being there and I loved every minute of it.

Our suburban home was a happy house back then. We had watched the construction from the basement up and moved in December 1970. It was one of the most exciting things we did as a family. Every weekend we would take a drive to see how much more of the house was built. We watched them pour the foundation and build the frame. We spotted the cut out holes that were to be windows or doors and we were filled with anticipation as the roof went on. Soon it was time to celebrate. We had a house. I remember the feeling of joy and love as Rodney and I stood in what was to be the family room, holding hands with the electricity of excitement pulsing between us. This was my fairy tale come true—our house, our family. We had had our problems, but I believed they were behind us and this was the life I had dreamed of ever since I could remember. Rodney worked very hard so we could buy that house. He spent three nights a week on call at the Military Medical Centre until we had enough money for the down payment. We were extremely happy family of five (Alex and James were not yet born).

Rodney rarely participated in the daily running of the house or child rearing. That was okay as my job was to take care of the whole family. I did not expect anything different. He was a very proud and loving father committed to his family, or so I thought.

Our entertainment was simple—a warm crackling log fire and a bottle of wine, even a smooch on the sofa after the kids had gone to bed. Our neighbours became our close friends and we entertained one another. One of my favourite winter evenings was the once-a-month lobster dinners we had with Mary and Colin, who lived across the street with their two girls and a boy (John, who was, and still is, William's best friend). Lobsters in 1971 cost less than two dollars a pound so although a treat, this was not as extravagant as it sounds. We alternated houses, and who bought the wine and who bought the lobsters.

The first time we did this, the guys sent Mary and I to the market to pick up the live lobsters. Now, I am not sure what we were thinking live lobsters looked like, but I do know that we were both surprised to see them so very active. The fishmonger was a rather grumpy looking man who didn't have much time for 'lobster- challenged' housewives. He just placed the live lobsters in a plastic bag inside a brown paper grocery bag, threw some fresh seaweed over the top and thrust the bag towards us. Perhaps it was the semi stifled gasps or the way we both lurched backwards as he handed us the bag of lobsters, that brought on a sudden and quite unexpected roar of laughter. I am not sure what frightened us more, the laughter or the lobsters, but after we had pulled ourselves together we too started to laugh.

The fishmonger reassured us that the lobsters could not climb out of the bag and, if kept cool, they would not move about. The reassuring words did not assuage our fears so, embarrassed and giggling like schoolgirls, we set off for home. We could hear the lobsters moving around in the bag. Our imaginations were somewhere in a B-rated horror movie waiting for an enormous claw to reach over the back seat and grab us by the neck That was the first and last time we ever picked up live lobsters. We designated the lobster pick up to the men.

I can still taste those fresh lobsters with lots of drawn butter (low-fat diets were not really an issue back then), warm crusty bread, with a glass, or two, of chilled white wine, preferably Black Tower. What a feast! We talked and laughed into the early hours of the morning.

Our street was full of friendly people and we supported one another. Sometimes it was building a fence or playroom, other times it was clearing the snow or babysitting. Our kids played together, as did the adults. We had some wonderful, often impromptu parties, barbecues in the summer because it was too hot to cook inside, fondues in the winter because a snowstorm had blocked the roads, or just because it was a bad week. It really didn't matter what the season or what the reason, we just liked to get together.

I remember one particularly brutal winter. It was freezing and the snow just kept coming and coming until we could no longer see over the snow banks. The driveways looked like burrows and the snow banks reached the second story windows, but winter was not finished yet. It was only February and a monster storm hit. The wind howled and it snowed for hours. Rodney was in the city delivering a baby when it started. His was the last car to drive down our street, thanks to his four-wheel drive. A couple of cars tried to follow in his tracks, but were abandoned as the snow reached above their axles. Even the four-wheel drive was not enough to get the Chevy Blazer up the driveway.

The next morning we were snowed in—no school or work — we couldn't move. Even the snowplows couldn't get through. It took us all day to dig out the abandoned cars and then we had to face the mammoth task of digging out the driveways and footpaths. By the time we finished the neighbourhood was a labyrinth with a maze of tall, narrow pathways running between the houses. The snow banks must have been 10 feet high. Even the tallest of our men could not see over them. That evening we made a potluck supper and gathered at the home of our immediate neighbours, Ian and Helen. Exhausted from the day's activities but re-energized by the food and company, we played Twister (a crazy 70s game) and finished up with Ian (who was of Scottish heritage) trying to teach us a Scottish jig using his ceremonial swords. I laugh just thinking about what we must have looked like and am thankful no toes were lost.

We laughed at our antics as we wound our way home through the maze of snow burrows. The wind had dropped. A few stray snowflakes drifted lazily to the ground as the moon pushed the last remaining cloud to one side. The sky twinkled with stars in the stillness, every sound muffled but the new falling snow. It was a beautiful night. I stopped at the front porch, held my breath, and tried to absorb the beauty and stillness of this winter's night.

Canadian winters are long and hard and although our friendships helped the winters pass a little faster, we were always pleased to see the snow melt and long cold nights turn into long hot summer days. Large sirloin steaks sizzled on barbecues, cold beer filled too many shelves in the fridge and kids laughed and squealed in the pool while overheated adults joined them in underwater games.

Once the children had settled in bed on hot humid nights, and preferably dark moonless ones, the grown-ups played their own pool games and were known to slip into the pool minus bathing suits. Skinny-dipping was risqué at the time. Our sinful behaviour was witnessed only by twinkling fireflies. Getting in and out of the water could be a challenge, but the excitement of doing something naughty was exhilarating. Keep in mind, the year was 1971—Blackburn Hamlet was home to respectable upper-middle-class suburbanites. By the way, ladies, I found it interesting that the women were always game to take the birthday suit plunge. The men, however, frequently chickened out. I wonder why? I should mention that most of us had not seen our thirtieth birthday and we were in good physical shape, in spite of the beer, steaks and butter.

Most of the neighbourhood get-togethers happened on the weekends and sometimes in the evening, except for one afternoon. A casual gathering of mothers and young kids met in Mary's backyard. It was a particularly hot, humid day and Mary offered the group a drink called Purple Passions, a long cold drink just right for such a day. It looked and tasted something like a grape slushy from the 7-Eleven stores. The purple juice slid down like cool refreshing lemonade, except Mary's version had quite the kick, not apparent until several glasses of juice had been consumed. Simple to make, Purple Passions consisted of grape juice, crushed ice and vodka, swished around in a blender and voila, purple passion. As the afternoon progressed, the proportion of grape juice to vodka got a little muddled, or perhaps a lot muddled, judging by the volume of laughter and crazy, mixed up conversations that bellowed from the backyard onto the street. It took our husbands by surprise as unheard car doors closed and weary, business suited men popped their heads into the Mary's backyard.

The hungry husbands found the incident quite amusing and willingly picked up KFC for supper, delighting the kids. Mothers relieved of their parental duties retired to sleep off the purple passions. Looking back, I think this was a very good de-stressor for all of us. In spite of their amusement, the men definitely let us know this was not to happen again. I liked living in this great community, Blackburn Hamlet, and I believed this life would go on happily ever after.

Rodney and I had had some problems in our eight or nine years of marriage, but right at that moment, things could not be better. In 1971 and 1972 two more children were born, Alex and James. Alex was planned because I loved babies and tended to get broody as they grew up. James was a bit of a surprise, but a very welcome one. Alex was only two months old when the doctor told me I was pregnant.

It was wonderful having the two little ones to raise together. Many people assumed we were devout Roman Catholics, but Rodney always put them straight, saying with great pride, "no, we are just passionate Protestants." He was also proud of the fact that as a medical doctor he earned good money and could afford to support and raise a large family. In the 70s, there was a shift in attitude toward smaller families. Two point five kids was the acceptable average for a manageable family. Some people thought that the world was overpopulated and that it was irresponsible to have more children. Many times we explained our reasons for such a large brood. It was so ironic that Rodney's sense of responsibility and passionate feelings toward his family could take such a drastic and fast turn.

In those early years in Blackburn Hamlet we were a traditional suburban family. I played house for real—cooking, washing, decorating, sewing, taking care of our children and all my husband's needs, great or small. It was just like my mother had taught me all those years ago. I was happy, living the dream. Rodney was a highly respected medical doctor with great potential for career advancement within the university and the Family Practice Unit. His income was more than adequate to comfortably raise even a large family. He worked hard and he too seemed happy and content. Our lifestyle, income and prospects were on target and realistic. Had things stayed that way, my dreams and expectations would most certainly have been met and probably exceed my vision of happily ever after. Like many dreams and fairy tales, the happiness bubble was about to burst.

5

Living with an Abusive Drunk

Taking a step back to 1960, the early days in northern England, I recall a saying: 'big hats and no drawers.' What this means is that someone's outer appearance is affluent, but the real situation is shallow and not what it appears. In the case of our suburban life, it appropriately referred to the appearance of perfect families and the contrast with what was really going on behind closed doors.

With my crown of denial firmly attached to my head, I pretended everything was fine and in the beginning it was okay, but things began to change and 'okay' became a long way from the truth. I was later to discover that we were not the only family in the neighbourhood to have 'big hats and no drawers.' At the time, all I could see were the 'big hats.'

Our secret was Rodney's drinking and abusive behaviour, both physical and emotional. The abuse was usually directed toward me, but sometimes the children felt the brunt of his moods. It may sound odd to call the drinking a secret because the neighbourhood, especially our street, loved to socialize and we could always find an excuse to get together. Rodney's drinking was more than social and I knew it, but the others did not. In the '70s, drinking even to excess was more socially acceptable than it is today. I was not the only one who made excuses for him. When I asked him to slow down, our friends would encourage him with comments like "Leave him alone, he's just enjoying himself." I knew better.

When I met Rodney in 1958, he was already a hardened drinker but I chose not to see it. We were both students, Rodney doing the second half of his medical degree and I was finishing my diploma in home economics. We studied and partied hard, just like everyone else. Medical students in particular had a reputation for wild parties. I remember one loud party. The record player was blasting Michael Row Your Boat Ashore. The phone rang for one of the young doctors. The comment from the senior doctor was, "Hurry up and get Michael's bloody boat ashore, you're needed in emergency!" This invoked peels of laughter including the senior doctor.

Rodney was one of the few students who drank to excess. He became verbally abusive the more he drank, especially if it was hard liquor. Whiskey was the worst. A hangover always produced remorse and apologies and a promise not to do it again. He could go for long periods of time without drinking, often promoted by lack of money or impending exams, but the drinking always returned. Having led a sheltered life, this bothered me. I had no idea how to handle it and even wondered if I was the cause. Excessive drinking was not something that happened in our family. I only ever recall seeing my mother drunk once and have no recollection of my father drinking. Instinct told me Rodney's behaviour was unacceptable but I was afraid to confront him. I pushed the concern away and convinced myself that I was overreacting. There seemed to be no history of alcoholism in the family. Rodney's parents were almost teetotalers. They only drink I ever saw them take was a glass of ginger wine at Christmas.

There was, however, an incident the first time I went to his parent's home. It wasn't about their drinking but their reaction to Rodney's. Because we lived in different cities, I was invited to spend the weekend with the family. All was going well. I seemed to hit it off with his parents and I bonded with his only sibling, an older sister. But they were still strangers to me so when Rodney announced he was meeting his old school friend Jack and I wasn't invited, I was not happy. Rodney promised he would not be long. Then we could do something for the rest of the evening.

I finally went to bed at midnight, angry and upset at being abandoned and, to add insult to injury, I had to listen to his mother making excuses for his absence. About two o'clock in the morning, I heard a great commotion in the hallway. Rodney was home and very drunk. I went to the top of the stairs to see him swaying, talking and laughing in a drunken stupor, not making any sense. He stumbled on the stairs and needed help to get up. Fortunately, his father had waited up for him. The commotion woke his mother who came out of her bedroom. I returned to my bed and listened, expecting to hear a reprimand. Instead, I heard her ask, "Did you have a good time with Jack? You must be tired? Off to bed now. Goodnight, son."

I was surprised by his mother's words but thought she probably did the right thing and she would talk to him in the morning."

I ate breakfast and waited for Rodney, trying to make conversation with people I did not know, who could quite possibly become my in-laws. Rodney slept through the morning and I knew that even when he woke he would be very hung-over. I was hurt, ashamed, embarrassed, angry and naively assumed his mother would feel the same way.

"I am sure you are as upset as I am about Rodney's behaviour last night." I expected support from his mother. What a mistake that was!

"How could you talk about Rodney that way?" she yelled at me in complete denial. "He wasn't drunk, he was just having a good time with his friends. He is a good boy and would never do anything like that."

I was stunned into silence. My gut feeling told me that this was not right. The fact that I was afraid to talk to anyone about it should have given me a clue. What can I say? I was naïve. I could hear my own mother's words, "Don't make a fuss, what would people think?" So I decided I was overreacting. After all he was just a student having fun. Rodney convinced me that he was quite normal. I believed him because I wanted it to be the truth, and I did not have enough confidence in myself to trust my own feelings.

Looking back, the warning signs were all there. Rodney was a man with a lot of problems. Hindsight is always 20/20, but had I acknowledged there was a problem and not denied my feelings in the beginning, things might have turned out very differently.

I finished college in 1960, two years before Rodney would graduate. My father found me a job working at the East Midlands Electricity Board so I went back home to live with my parents. We were now living in different cities about 60 miles apart, absence making the heart grow fonder. We became engaged to be married in the spring of 1961, missed each other terribly and the time we shared was magic. Our world was going to be perfect; we were so much in love. I can still feel the warmth of his arms around my shoulders, holding me tightly, my heart skipping a beat, butterflies in my stomach and those eyes; how I remember the soft, loving gaze as we looked into each other's eyes. If Rodney was drinking during those two years, I was too far away both in body and mind to know about it.

We were married September 1, 1962, right after Rodney graduated from medical school.

Our first child, Nathan, was born nine months and two days after we were married. That had folks counting the months on their fingers, which amused us. In the '60s, if a girl became pregnant out of wedlock, as they delicately put it, she either "had to get married" which meant the baby was two or three months premature or she was secretly whisked off to take care of an elderly aunt, and would reappear nine months later. Because my waistline quickly expanded, they assumed we had to get married, which was ridiculous as we had been planning this wedding for two years. Even a hint of impropriety would set off a round of gossip and there was plenty of that going around as my belly grew.

Married life was good at first. Rodney worked hard doing his internship and residency, and I was very content as a new mother. Our lives revolved around the hospital. As the ward doctor, Rodney was expected to go and carve the turkey for his patients on Christmas Day. Each ward was given a roasted turkey with all the trimmings. The head nurse always had sherry hidden behind screens at the corner of each ward, waiting to wish doctors a Merry Christmas as they did their morning rounds. The number of wards a doctor had was directly related to how 'merry' Christmas was.

Nathan was six months old. I pushed him around the wards in his stroller and he lapped up all the attention from nurses and patients. As the doctor's wife, I was treated with a great deal of kindness and respect, both nurses and patients appreciating our visit. Our motive was to be together as a family on Christmas Day. The bonus was the love and appreciation we felt from the patients and nurses. It was a wonderful, giving way to spend Christmas Day. This was our normal Christmas Day until Rodney went into private practice.

6

Terrifying Highs - Debilitating Lows

Rodney accepted his first position as a family physician in Sheffield, Yorkshire, assistant to Dr. Shaw, a well established GP (General practitioner). Dr. Shaw had been practicing family medicine for over 40 years and was now in his 70s, preparing to retire. Working under and learning from such an experienced doctor with the possibility of taking over the practice in a few short years made our future look bright.

The position came with a beautiful, old Victorian home, which Dr. Shaw had lived in years ago. The surgery office was attached to the house and I remember opening the heavy oak door for the first time and being in awe at the magnificent oak staircase. I imagined Victorian ladies sweeping down the stairs in their long flowing gowns. The house had six bedrooms, four reception rooms, a separate staircase leading to the maids' quarters, stables and a coach house.

Far from being a palace, the house had not been lived in for 15 years. We set to work and peeled off at least 10 layers of wallpaper. The last layer was a 1902 newspaper and we spent quite some time reading the news and laughing at the old ads. We cleaned and painted enough rooms to live in and closed off the rest of the house.

Dr. Shaw was an old school doctor and although the surgery area was used every day, it had this Dickensian look about it. The waiting room was paneled in dark oak and lined with hard wooden chairs. The centre of the doctor's office featured an enormous oak desk, three overstuffed leather chairs and thick, dusty medical books filled the antique bookcases set against the walls. The old wood, dusty books and leather, together with a hint of antiseptic, gave off a strange musty smell.

The most intriguing part of the house was the dispensary. Dr. Shaw still dispensed his own prescriptions; he didn't trust pharmacists. Time had stood still. It was a perfect Victorian apothecary. The walls were lined ceiling to floor with oak cupboards. Through the glass doors, you could see blue and brown jars and bottles in all shapes and sizes. On the marble counter, there were mortars and pestles to grind down ingredients, tiny scales and measuring spoons ready for the delicate task of making the medicine, mostly cough syrups or tonics (the kind that cured whatever ails you). The recipe book, although large, was a little vague as Dr. Shaw had most of the formulas committed to memory, which was fine so long as he was in town. The inevitable happened. While Dr. Shaw was on vacation, old Mrs. Drew came in for her tonic. The recipe gave the ingredients but not the proportions. Rodney asked for the old bottle and whatever was left inside. He mixed what he thought would be the appropriate amounts, tasted it and then held both bottles up to the light to see if they matched. Once they tasted and looked the same, Rodney handed Mrs. Drew her tonic. About two weeks later, Mrs. Drew, who had been quite upset at having to see the young doctor, on this occasion she specifically requested *that nice young doctor*. Older patients generally liked to stay with their own doctor, so we were curious to know why Mrs. Drew wanted to switch.

Soon it became apparent. It was the tonic. It may have tasted and smelled the same, but it was twice as strong. Mrs. Drew felt much better having had a happy two weeks on the young doctor's elixir. Upon Dr. Shaw's return, it was discovered that Rodney had added a double dose of most potent ingredient. The next bottle was mixed with the correct proportions. Whether Mrs. Drew noticed we never found out.

Less than a year after we moved to Sheffield, life became a roller coaster ride, highs of wonderful happiness and lows of despair. With tentative anticipation, Rodney would climb back up to happiness only to dive back down into misery. I was to discover, much later, that Rodney had a problem not only with alcohol but also with severe bouts of depression, which he never acknowledged and was a master at hiding. The drinking started innocently. We didn't go out very much as I was pregnant with Katrina. Rodney was always on call, and we had very little money back then. Rodney decided to make his own beer, small batches at first, which turned out quite well. But the quantity was too small for a drinking man so he bought a 20-gallon plastic garbage can to brew the beer in. The beer was prepared and fermented in the kitchen. Fermenting beer smells thick and heavy like a very pungent sourdough gone off. This stench permeated the entire house for weeks. Once the brew was bottled, the smell disappeared, but he drank it as fast as he brewed it so the next batch was ready to go within days of bottling. The bottles were now one-gallon jugs. The more that was brewed, the more was consumed, and consume he did. A drink with dinner became many drinks before, after and during dinner. He became moody, lethargic and argumentative. I was afraid to speak and began to creep about the house.

One morning around nine o'clock, I noticed Rodney was in the living room and I reminded him it was past nine and his patients were waiting. I stopped abruptly at the doorway as I saw him swing the gallon jug up to his shoulder resting it on his arm so he could drink the beer directly from the jug. I was terrified. How could I ignore this behaviour? Drinking before work and out of one-gallon jugs was definitely excessive drinking and his frightening mood swings were not normal but I could no longer distinguish between normal and abnormal.

Ashamed and embarrassed, I dared not speak to anyone, so I made up my own little world. I worked harder, tried harder, took all the blame and tried to make things right. It was my fault. I was not a good wife, housekeeper or mother to our son. I had many reasons but no solutions. I began to cover up for his drinking and hangovers, constantly making excuses for him, and even began to believe some of those excuses.

It became more difficult to predict Rodney's mood swings that could be raging anger or gentle thoughtfulness and everything in between. When our son was only three months old, I discovered I was pregnant, happy with the news, if somewhat surprised Rodney was excited and understanding. I miscarried the baby and he was so loving, gentle and caring. He took great care of me and Nathan. But when my beloved grandmother, Nana, passed away, he became cruel and unsympathetic. Nana had been a large part of my childhood and I was heartbroken when she died but all he did was berate me for 'blubbering,' as he called my tearful grief.

I learned to suppress my emotions and found myself 'walking on eggshells.' I developed a kind of radar, constantly scanning for his mood changes and quickly adapting my responses to avoid his scathing remarks or abusive hand, particularly as I was pregnant again.

Quite suddenly, Rodney decided that he needed a change. He acknowledged he was stressed out and drinking too much. In his mind, Dr. Shaw, and the archaic practice, were to blame. In retrospect, I think patients had complained about his tardiness during surgery hours and I'm sure his alcohol breath and even drunken behaviour had come into question. I am not sure if Dr. Shaw fired him or gave him an ultimatum. Whatever happened, Rodney began applying for GP positions near his hometown and accepted a practice in Stockport where both his father and sister lived. Katrina was due to be born one week after we moved. Rodney had arrangements for me to give birth in Stockport but that was not to be. There are three things in life we have no control over: births, deaths and taxes. Katrina was born the day before we were due to move from Sheffield.

Rodney, Nathan and all our worldly belongings moved to Stockton with my mother looking after everything. In 1965, it was not unusual to be in hospital five or more days after a birth. I was so exhausted that they kept me in hospital for ten days before I was allowed to travel to my new home.

The move to Stockport was a good one. The drinking subsided, the mood swings leveled off and life seemed to be returning to normal. The Stockport family practice was busy, two surgeries a day, morning and evening, and house calls in between, and of course, we were on call 24 hours a day. I was receptionist and nurse, as well as doctor's wife and mother to our children. The patients liked us and the practice grew large enough to take on a partner, which meant Rodney could take some days and evenings off.

With more time on his hands, Rodney started going to the pub for the odd pint, which was harmless at first, until I started noticing some mood changes. His words were becoming more abrasive and hurtful, often covered by teasing, pretending he was joking. Just as I had begun to relax, the old fears returned, as did the drinking binges. The toughest part was not knowing what to expect. If he was in a good mood, it could be a happy binge, but most of the time it was an aggressive, combative binge.

Rodney had a massive chip on his shoulder. He was mad with the world and took his anger out on me: the dinner was cold, the house was a mess, the kids too noisy and no one could do anything right. The verbal abuse escalated and the physical abuse started. A threatening gesture, a little slap, nothing much at first—until one summer evening.

The children were in bed and I had settled in to watch TV. Rodney decided to go to bed early and that was fine except he wanted me to go with him. I made no attempt to move which made him very angry. The next thing I knew, he grabbed my very long brown hair and pulled me out of the chair toward the stairs. Imagine a loving child dragging a favourite rag doll upstairs, the doll bouncing on each stair. Except this was an angry drunken man and I was the rag doll. My hair was coming out at the roots, my arms and legs were slapping up against the spindles of the banister, my hips and ribs were burning from being scraped against the carpet and bruised from hitting each step. He released his grip when we reached the bedroom. I was crying and sobbing so hard I couldn't speak. Although I had some physical pain, my tears were of humiliation.

Suddenly, he reached out and grabbed my arm, pressing his fingers deep into my flesh. I froze, certain I was dead. Just as suddenly, he released his grip and tenderly pulled me into his arms. Stroking my hair, he leaned in, kissed me on the cheek and whispered, "I am sorry. I didn't want to hurt you, but if you had come when I asked this would not have happened." I was so relieved that his anger had abated; I said nothing, knowing that to argue would only trigger another rage. After the rag doll incident, Rodney calmed down and I avoided any kind of conflict, especially if he had been drinking and my radar was on high alert for mood swings.

7

The Nightmare Comes True

Rodney's remorse appeared genuine and, after a two-month dry spell (he'd even managed to stay sober over the Christmas holidays), I let my guard down. As New Year's Eve 1968 approached, we had planned a romantic evening together. The children were in bed and I was cooking a special dinner of roast duck.

Rodney disappeared just as I was about to serve dinner, saying he'd be back soon he had a surprise for me. What a surprise! He came home at 11:30, drunk as a skunk, after spending the evening in the pub. Anger doesn't even describe how I felt. I was beside myself with worry. The dinner was ruined, as was New Year's Eve.

For the first time I decided it was time to leave, just temporarily. Teach him a lesson, I thought. After some angry shouting I got in my car, and with tears streaming down my face, I started to drive home to my parents. My parents lived in Nottingham, about 60 miles from Stockport. While wiping away my tears, I thought: *You know, Susan, leaving him need not be temporary. I could come back tomorrow and pick up the children. Daddy would help me.* But then I remembered my Dad's words after my wedding, "Now you are married, you have a husband to care for you. No need to come running home." This thought brought me to tears again. His words were a way of letting go of his little girl, but in that moment I felt as though I would be letting him down by going home. I was married and had a life with my husband.

Rodney's drinking and abuse was not a trivial thing but my parents did not know about it because I had chosen not to tell them. Thinking of my dad brought on more tears. He was a kind, gentle soul and I suspect he had doubts about Rodney. I had seen it in his eyes, but he would never interfere unless I asked for help. But that didn't stop him asking if I was all right. The weeping had reached hysteria and I pulled the car off the road and reached for a hankie (before the days of Kleenex). As I leaned over to get the hankie from my handbag I saw the fuel gauge, the needle was close to empty. Realizing I would not make it to Nottingham brought on another wave of tears. Sobbing, I headed back home thinking, *Well at least he will have had a scare and will worry about me. Now he will understand.* The joke was on me. He hadn't even noticed I was gone. This hurt far more than the ruined New Year's Eve. Sadly, I was not taken seriously and we laughed about my attempt to leave, thwarted by my poor planning.

However, in retrospect, I have often wondered if my attempt to leave, had in fact frightened Rodney because he stopped drinking and, once again our day-to-day life went back to normal. Rodney started to talk about making a career move. Unsure if family medicine was what he wanted, he began to investigate going back to school to study psychiatry. Having decided to make a career move, we decided it should be a big move, not just another county or city but another country. Within six months, Rodney had a residency position at St. John's Mental Hospital in Newfoundland, Canada. We sold our house, packed our belonging and our three children and immigrated to Canada. I was in heaven. My mother was born in Canada, so for me it was like coming home, albeit St John's was a little different to Toronto and it was debatable how Canadian Newfoundland was at the time.

There were two things that I should have seen but did not. In my defense, I was only twenty-eight years old. I had three kids, ages, six, four and 18 months and an unstable husband so I tried whatever I could to make my family life normal.

The first thing I discovered was that Newfoundlanders love to party and drink (and enjoy Screech, a very potent rum). Rodney had found his heaven here too. He quickly and easily fell right in with some serious drinking pals and life was one big party.

The second thing I might have guessed but didn't realize was that studying psychiatry only fuelled Rodney's tendency for depression and mental illness. It wasn't long before Rodney was as sick and depressed as his patients. My dream life had turned into a nightmare, worse than anything I had experienced.

Living with a drunk is difficult because you live on adrenaline, constantly on guard, prepared for something to happen. After a while, I recognized the signs and played my cards as skillfully as I knew how. But when you add clinical depression and suicide threats, it was like living with a loose cannon. If he was not in a rage, lashing out at everyone and everything, he was lying motionless, staring into space, drinking to feel something, or drinking to dull the pain. The only constant was that I never knew what might happen next.

Looking back, I find it amazing that we still partied with friends and, if I voiced concern, I was told 'he's just having fun.' Considering these friends were in as bad a shape as Rodney, the response was to be expected. Even more surprising is that Rodney's colleagues at the hospital didn't see that he had a problem.

Once again, Queen of Denial, placed her crown on her head and pretended everything was normal. Instead of listening to my instincts and trusting that I was right to be concerned, I convinced myself (with some help from Rodney) that I was the problem and I worked even harder to put things right. He had me so convinced that I was over anxious and overreacting that I allowed him to prescribe the anti-anxiety drug, Librium, to help calm me. I probably benefited from the medication, but the wrong person was being treated.

The solution was another move. Believe it or not, I did not see the pattern, but in retrospect I realize that every time Rodney hit the bottle hard and finished in the depths of depression, his way out was to escape from the job and move. This latest move was to Ottawa and back into family practice, but this time teaching family practice at the University of Ottawa. Rodney had a prestigious position, excellent pay and a new lease on life in many ways. That was how we finished up in Blackburn Hamlet. We came so close to the fairy tale life and we even lived it for a few years.

Our normal happy life in Ottawa was showing signs of the 'big hat, no draws life.' Rodney's carefully hidden mood swings were evident and often resulted in physical or verbal abuse directed at Katrina or myself. Katrina often got the worst of it. She was an outspoken child and arguments would escalate into spankings that were more like beatings as Rodney lost his temper. I intervened frequently, although I wasn't always successful. The boys didn't get the same physical abuse. They were tormented in a different way. I remember Nathan being dragged out of bed at two o'clock in the morning because he had forgotten to put his bike away. He yelled at the boys for no reason or cooked up a reason only known to Rodney. He'd yell, "You know why you are being punished," when they had no idea what he was talking about, or he would ask them very obscure questions and then berate them for not knowing the answers.

He was drinking again, but not before breakfast. I could handle the moods and temper, so the Queen of Denial let things slide. Anyone who has lived with a drunk knows the pattern. It appears harmless at first. He is in a good mood, with a sometimes forced, happy-go-lucky attitude. As the drink takes hold, the mood swings to aggressive sarcasm followed by vicious torments and teasing. I sat through endless hours of talking or arguing about nothing. I cringed from the slaps either on me or the table and tried not to cry from the hurtful words and teasing. I dared not argue or even respond, because if I said the wrong thing, he would lose his temper. I was deathly afraid for my safety and for the children's.

I spent a great deal of time protecting the children from his temper so they were usually in bed or out of reach. I nodded and smiled in agreement with everything he said. At opportune moments, I suggested he was tired and ought to go to bed. If I was lucky, I could get him upstairs before he passed out. If not, I am sure it was quite a comical scene as this five-foot two-inch woman tried to maneuver a 275-pound, six-foot man up the stairs. The alternative was to leave him on the couch. At least I would have the bed to myself and get some sleep for a change.

Sleeping with Rodney was like sleeping with an old wino. He smelled of stale booze and I was never sure if he was going to vomit or pee all over me. If he made it out of bed, there was a good chance he'd pass out before or after getting to the bathroom. Then getting the moron back into bed was a challenge. I spent many sleepless nights either hanging off the edge of our bed or on the living room couch waiting for a thud from the master bedroom.

I felt exhaustion and pain every day, all day, an abnormality that had become normal. My stomach hurt from being tied in knots, and my throat was tight from always being on the brink of tears. Some days it was hard to keep going and most days I wondered how I did.

The mornings always brought a new day. He would say, "I don't know what happened, I am really sorry, it won't happen again." I believe he sincerely meant what he said. Then he'd put his arms around me. I'd stand like a statue, repulsed by his affection and frightened. But, I'd smiled and say, "please promise me it will not happen again." He would promise and life went on until the next time and there would be a next time. I just prayed we would have a reprieve for a day or two and that depended on how remorseful he felt.

I had accepted or more accurately rationalized this way of life as normal. Things couldn't get any worse, or could they? Things got worse. Physicians have access to all kinds of drugs and Rodney started mixing prescription drugs with the alcohol. He took hallucinogenic sleeping pills to help him sleep, amphetamines to wake him up and valium to calm his nerves.

I was aware of this new behaviour but not aware of the severity until I received a call from the pharmacist questioning the amount of medication I was taking. I told him I wasn't taking any medication, suggesting he had the wrong name and phone number. He assured me it was my name and address on the prescription. I suggested he call the doctor to clarify the name. There was even more humiliation when I realized that Rodney was writing prescriptions in my name to feed his addiction. I was furious and confronted him that night. He crumbled at the accusations and pleaded with me that he needed the drugs to get through the day and I believed him. He agreed not to use my name for his prescriptions and promised to cut down and be careful. That I did not believe. I watched him like a hawk but I had no way of knowing what he was taking or how much. I suspect he continued to use my name but used different pharmacists to cover his tracks.

Perhaps it was my watchful eye that caused him to begin going out in the evenings. He frequently stayed late at work, returning home in the early hours of the morning. Now my sleeplessness was due to pacing up and down, staring out of the big bay window in the living room, waiting. Knowing he was drunk and high, driving at speed along the Queensway, I was afraid he might kill himself or worse, some innocent person on the highway. Fortunately, he always made it home and to my amazement was never stopped by the police. One bitterly cold winter night, he arrived home on foot because the car was stuck in a snow bank. He had made it into Blackburn Hamlet but had turned down the wrong street. He couldn't remember where he left the car and it took us an hour to find it.

8

Could Life Get Any Worse?

Driving was a major issue, whether it was trying to take the keys from him after a party or making a judgment call whether it was safe for the children to go with him on a camping trip.

Rodney's favourite pastime was camping and canoeing in the wilderness. I did not share his passion for the outdoors. I hate bugs, long grass, swimming in weedy lakes and communal bathrooms and it always rained. The kids enjoyed it and I felt it was good for them to be outdoors. I tolerated camping until the night we had a huge thunderstorm and I woke up to a river gushing under our tent. We had camped on a dried out riverbed. So I rarely went camping after that.

Rodney took the older children on weekend trips, leaving me at home with the babies and modern household conveniences. These trips were therapeutic for Rodney. They helped him relax and the children enjoyed the time with their dad, or so I thought.

I became suspicious one hot Friday afternoon that he was not coping with these camping trips. Rodney was in a particularly foul mood, often an indication that he needed a fix.

While he was changing, I searched the car for alcohol or drugs and found a 12-pack of beer, a bottle of Scotch, a stash of sleeping pills, Valium and other pills under the driver's seat. Horrified at the thought of the kids alone in the wilderness with this sick man I knew what had to be done. Terrified or not, I had to confront him. The safety of the children came first. I could not let them go on the trip.

Rodney surprised me. He didn't lose his temper or even put up a fight. He simply got in the car and left on his own. I have since heard stories of sleeping bags floating in flooded tents while he slept dry and comfortable in the car, incidents of overturned canoes resulting in near drowning, and the children did not enjoy these trips as I had assumed. It delighted them when they stopped.

Rodney's social graces were lacking, possibly because of his upbringing, but there were social events we were obliged to attend—fancy cocktail parties, elaborate dinner parties—the kind of functions Rodney hated. He always felt inferior and uncomfortable so he did what he knew best to relieve the discomfort—he drank. The drinks usually flowed at these functions and my radar was on high alert, ready to tune into the warning signs and get him out before he made a fool of himself.

On one occasion, Dr. Carter and his wife were entertaining a group of us from the university. We had just finished a magnificent dinner and were invited to enjoy coffee and liqueurs in the living room. I was admiring the antique furniture, the art collection and the plush white carpet. Beautiful but not what I would call a family home and they obviously had no kids.

I must have disconnected my radar for a while and had not noticed that Rodney was knocking back the brandy. It was too late to get him out. My suggestions of getting home for the babysitter were falling on drunk ears, and I feared that if I insisted he would become belligerent. Then it happened. He stood up and began to weave his way across the living room saying, "I don't feel too good." As the words came out, so did the vomit all over the white carpet. Our host and hostess were very gracious as I offered to get the carpet cleaned and apologized every way I knew how for Rodney's behaviour. How do you say 'sorry' for something like that? They made excuses for him, told me it wasn't my fault and reassured me that sometimes these things happen. Even today I feel the shame of that night.

I don't recall the fall out. I doubt there were anymore invitations. Our social life, other than neighbourly get-togethers, dwindled and, at the time, I thought it was Rodney being antisocial but on reflection I suspect we were no longer included.

Home was no haven. I walked on eggshells, waiting for the next bad mood or drinking binge. He now hated my going out in the evening so I limited this to the occasional PTA meeting and bridge with the neighbours every second Tuesday. Paranoia crept into Rodney's psyche. I was reprimanded for going out and interrogated about who I was with and how long I would be gone.

The paranoia reached its worst on one of my bridge nights at Diane's house. Diane's living room was directly across the street from our house. You could see right into her living room from ours.

Rodney phoned every hour to ask who I was with and when I would be home. It was embarrassing for me as every call disturbed the bridge game. He finally stopped calling but was lying in wait in the front hall when returned home. The first thing I felt was my head cracking against the doorframe, followed by a string of verbal abuse. I tried to explain that we were playing cards and I had spent some extra time talking. He brushed past me, poured a drink and walked upstairs screaming at me that he couldn't take care of the kids. I foolishly looked up and asked, "why not? They are your kids too." Enraged, he threw the drink in my face.

My eyes stung from the alcohol and my head throbbed from the crack on the door. I was the closest I had ever been to leaving him. I remember planning how I would wake up the children and get them into the car. I was terrified of what might happen if he heard us. Judging by his earlier rage, he would kill me and hurt the kids. Even to this day, I cannot put into words the despair I felt that night.

Even if I managed to get away there was nowhere to go with five children, no money and no family. I wasn't aware of any safe houses. This was the mid 70s, so I'm not sure they existed at that time. Even the law did not protect me. It considered wives chattel. If I walked out, there was a strong chance I would not be allowed back in the home. And, hadn't I made a promise 'for better or worse, in sickness and health'? I had to work things out, but how?

After the drink in the face, I was a wreck. I needed to talk to someone I could trust. I decided to talk to my friend Jackie. Our children went to school together and our husbands worked in the same department at the university. She was a counselor at the Distress Centre so I thought she would understand my problem.

Jackie was shocked at my story and assured me that I was not the problem. I was being abused. I don't recall any advice, just the relief of being able to talk to someone, and Jackie was a very good listener. Part of me was still in denial, but Jackie made me see the first glimmer of truth that Rodney was in deep trouble. She offered her help and support, which I declined. Sharing my secret made me feel better and everything would be fine."

Rodney's erratic behaviour at home made me wonder how he functioned at work. After all, he worked with five physicians. Surely they could tell something was wrong? Why didn't they talk to me? Was he keeping it together at work?

Two days later, Jackie called to ask if I was alone and could she pop over to see me. I answered yes to both. I had my answer to the work question. Rodney was not functioning at work and the code of silence amongst his peers had been broken. His colleagues could no longer cover for him or ignore the drinking and drug taking. He was incapable of treating his patients. John, Jackie's husband, had been asked by the head of the department to speak with Rodney. Jackie wanted my permission to tell John what we had talked about earlier. Although I had spoken to her in confidence, she thought it was a good idea for John to understand what had been going on and I agreed with her. I dared to think I might get some help.

John and Rodney had a long talk. Amongst other things, they made it very clear to Rodney that if he didn't smarten up he would be out of a job. It was suggested that he take a two-week vacation to straighten himself out.

The combination of John's talk, a vacation, and the very real threat of losing his job, even the possibility of loosing his medical license, jolted Rodney into reality. He stopped drinking immediately and cut back on the drugs, using them only as prescribed by another doctor. Rodney's mood became somber and passive, no highs or lows. He was back at work and becoming more affectionate toward me. He was genuinely sorry for his past behaviour and I no longer feared for our safety. I dared to think that life might just work out and we would be okay.

The past events, however, had taken their toll. I felt no passion for Rodney, neither love nor hate. I stayed neutral at all times, happy to have a stable life again. I began to trust a little more each day, although I never let my guard down. I always had this little voice inside saying, 'Be Careful.'

Over time life did return to normal and in August 1977 we piled the kids into the Chevy Blazer with camping gear (yes, you heard me correctly) and set off for a two-week trip. Rodney had promised we would stay in decent campsites with running water and if I didn't feel like cooking, we would eat out. If there was any sign of bad weather or other problems, we would go to a motel and if I felt I couldn't cope, we would go home. He kept his promises. We had a wonderful trip until the weather turned terrible and true to his promise, we stayed in a motel. When the weather didn't improve, we drove home a couple of days earlier.

I was falling in love again and we were a family once more. We had been here before but I was beginning to allow myself thoughts of happiness.

Two months later, November 1977, was to be 'That Fateful Day.' After all, I had put up with: the drinking, the drugs, the abuse, the pain and heartache, how dare he leave me? But leave me he did and now I faced the challenge of single motherhood.

9

The Separation Honeymoon

Once I was over the shock, I felt relief. The nightmare was over but it still took Rodney two months to move out. We decided he should stay until after Christmas for the sake of the children and for his birthday in January. I realized the delayed parting suited Rodney and why wouldn't it? He had declared his freedom. His girlfriend was across many oceans in South Africa, and I was his maid, cook, housekeeper and nanny. We even slept in the same bed, which in retrospect I find hard to believe. You could have driven a truck between us but, even so, it felt weird and I was uncomfortable with the arrangement.

The relief was short lived. My life was on hold and it was difficult to know how to behave. We were still husband and wife to the children, who had not been told of our separation, nor had we told our friends. At the same time I was trying to make plans to move into a strange single world, with the ever-watchful eyes of my ex-partner observing my every move. The excuses were numerous until finally I asked him to leave. He reluctantly found an apartment and told everyone I had thrown him out of the house. If that made him feel better, I could live with it; as long as he left. Unfortunately, it was also the story he told the children. I was to discover, much later, that Katrina believed that I was the one who broke up the family. This lie would create problems in my relationship with my daughter for years to come.

I looked for work. I am not sure of my motives at that time. Maybe I was being a martyr, or exercising my need to find independence or my instinct to provide for my children. Perhaps it was all of the above. Looking back, parenting five children alone was a demanding enough job, without adding work outside the home. I rationalized that Rodney should support the children but he didn't need to support me; a decision I would later regret.

I had been out of the workforce many years and working outside the home had never been a consideration. What could I do? I had no skills or recent work experience and I needed to take care of the children. The work I had been trained for didn't exist. There were no opportunities related to domestic science. I registered for a real estate course and learned how to sell homes. After all, I had run a home for 16 years. I had some selling experience from before I was married and I enjoyed being with people. The course was inexpensive. I could be working in a few short weeks from home with flexible hours. It sounded perfect, except that real estate agents work on straight commission and it would be a long time before I received a paycheque.

Taking my independence a little too far at this point, I wanted nothing from Rodney. I could do it all myself. As a result, I sold myself short, very short, and established a precedent that followed me through life.

My advice to any woman who finds herself in this situation: Take the time—all the time you need—to weigh all your options. Look at the long term as well as the short term. Think beyond raising the children. Raising children takes 20 to 30 years, depending on how many children you have. Putting the years into perspective, raising children is only half of your adult life. What are you going to do with the second half?

The wisest thing I could have done was to go back to school and work toward a university degree. My choice would have been psychology or education, maybe even a combination. Several things stopped me, most of them of my own doing. My self-esteem was at an all-time low and I had no confidence in my abilities. What I needed was a good friend to encourage me with words like, 'Just get off your butt and do it,' but at the time I was not confiding in anyone. I could only see the negatives. I didn't have the money to finance tuition and it never occurred to me that this could have been one of the stipulations in our separation agreement, or that I could have applied for a grant or loan.

I repeat, take the time to consider all your options, and I cannot emphasize enough the importance of friends, especially female friends. Their support, understanding and encouragement are worth a ton of gold. I didn't talk to my friends at first because I was ashamed of what had happened. I didn't take the time to consider all my options. Beyond the low self-esteem and lack of confidence was the feeling of not deserving, so I wouldn't ask Rodney or anyone to help me through school.

If I am truthful, I will admit that I was afraid to ask for anything. I just hoped I would get what I needed. I was always making 'do' with what came my way. I cannot stress strongly enough the importance of asking for what you need and want. I am not suggesting you become greedy or unreasonable, and of course, compromises are inevitable, but it is important that you consider yourself and voice your needs. If you don't ask, how will anyone know what you need? Most people are not mind readers.

During this time Rodney was feeling the reality of leaving his wife and five children and developed a guilty conscience. He was very generous financially and an amicable period evolved, the 'separation honeymoon.' The fighting and arguing stopped and he was genuinely concerned for our welfare. I only felt relief. There was no more walking on eggshells. Adapting to this new lifestyle was different, almost an adventure. I hated any kind of conflict, so settling into this amicable relationship was just fine.

We drew up an acceptable separation agreement. I was to have the house and contents. He took a few items of furniture and left the rest for me. We had two cars, the Chevy Blazer, which was his car and I took the Chevy station wagon. He took what money we had in the savings account and investments (I discovered much, much later that was a bad move as there was considerably more money than I was led to believe). He agreed to pay me $1,500 per month child support. A little piece of advice regarding money, support payments can disappear, as they did for me. If you have the option for a combination of lower support payments and a lump sum, I would suggest you consider it. If the payments cease, you have something to fall back on, and if the payments continue, you have the start of an education or retirement fund.

Rodney settled into a bachelor lifestyle and bought a bungalow about 45 miles away in rural Quebec. Country living had never appealed to me. I had visions of being stuck in the middle of nowhere with five young children and an unstable drunk. This was a dream come true for Rodney and he was stable and happy. The cottage was a small bungalow built into the side of a hill, surrounded by trees and shrubs with a wonderful view of a large pristine lake. The children spent every second weekend with him and they enjoyed the lake and the freedom of the outdoors.

The first winter was an 'eye opener' to Rodney. Even with a four-wheel-drive vehicle, snowstorms and temperatures dropping to minus 40 degrees centigrade, made commuting difficult. He started to look for places to stay in the city and he even thought it would be a great idea to stay at my place. He had it all worked out. He would sleep on the couch and this would be a great opportunity to spend time with the children. Fortunately, I had the good sense to say no.

It amazed me at how Rodney was getting his life together. He was happy and sober, at least around me. Lulled into a false sense of security, I even began to ponder the idea that if some changes were made there might be a possibility of our getting back together.

Some subtle changes came about though, small ones in Rodney's behaviour. He spent more time in the city and little time at his cottage, which meant he was spending less time with the children. I figured there was another girlfriend in the picture. The girlfriend in South Africa seemed to have fallen by the wayside, so I suspected the romance was over or he was two-timing the girlfriend now. I brushed it off. There was no reason he shouldn't have girlfriends, we were separated and he owed me nothing. He still loved his kids. What difference would it make? The kids would always come first. After all, I dated occasionally and I always put the kids first.

True to the typical double standard, when Rodney realized I was dating, he became jealous. He didn't want me but he didn't want me seeing other men either. The pretense was that I was naïve, not very worldly, he didn't trust the 'other' guys. He was concerned about the influence my dating might have on the children. In retrospect, he was right on both counts but his motive was jealousy.

What happened next had the biggest influence on my decision to break all ties and accept the fact that the marriage was over. Deep inside, I had harboured the thought that maybe one day things would change. On this day I knew they would not.

Rodney wanted to see me. He called and asked me to meet him at his place in Quebec, so we could talk alone. After much thought, I accepted his invitation. He had given me no clue as to what he wanted to talk about and I had no idea what to expect. I was nervous and the memories of his temper and violent mood swings were still fresh in my mind. Meeting him alone at his cottage in the middle of nowhere did not seem to be a smart thing to do, but he talked me into it. I remember my inner voice saying, 'Be careful, this is not a good idea,' and then my emotional self saying, 'It's okay, don't worry.'

It was a beautiful sunny September day. I had the good sense to go in daylight. There was a slight chill of fall in the air and the leaves were just beginning to change colour. As I pulled the car into the tree-covered driveway, I could see the sun shimmering on the lake. It really was a magnificent place.

Taking a deep breath, I stepped out of the car and walked toward the front door. Before I rang the doorbell, Rodney opened the door and greeted me warmly. It was a little awkward at first. My heart was pounding and my throat was very tight. I feared that if I spoke no sound would come out, so I just smiled. He gave me the grand tour of the cottage and that broke the ice and we both relaxed.

We sat in the sparsely furnished living room. The warmth from the wood stove took the chill out of the air and made the room cozy. We made polite conversation and I found myself getting impatient wondering when he would get to the point. He talked about the children and how he missed them. Then, without warning, he blurted out that he wanted to come home. I was stunned. It had never occurred to me that he was even thinking of coming home. He definitely had a plan. His words were: "I don't expect it to happen overnight. We could start dating again. We could date for a month or two and then I could move back home." As he was speaking, I was repeating in my head 'Dating again — what planet is he on?'

He continued, "The children just love the cottage so we would keep this for the summer and weekends, our home away from home."

I was speechless. I just stared at him like an idiot with my mouth wide open. With tears in his eyes he went on to say, "I am truly sorry for all the things I have done. I really have stopped drinking. I am a changed man and I promise things will be different." His performance deserved an Oscar and I could feel myself being sucked in. It sounded oh so tempting. Life would be back to normal, 'Was my fairy tale in reach again or was this an olive branch that would snap the moment he moved back home?'

Quite suddenly I became aware of my own feelings. I did not want any kind of reconciliation. The damage had been done. I no longer loved this man. I could not see the day when the hurt and pain he had inflicted on me would heal. I knew the trust had gone and it would never return.

My inner voice spoke to me loud and clear, and although I was not able to be completely honest, I could cautiously voice some of my inner thoughts. My stomach doing flip-flops, my voice barely more than a squeak, I said, "I really appreciate the many changes you have made and you seem so much happier these days, but I think it is too soon to talk of reconciliation. I am not ready for such a big step." I then rationalized my statement by saying, "Waiting for a few months, even a year, is a small portion of our lives and I want to be absolutely sure we are doing the right thing." Rodney nodded in partial agreement, but told me he really wanted to get on with his life. The pleasant meeting was ending as Rodney revealed his hidden agenda.

Although we had been together for nearly twenty years, Rodney could still surprise me and catch me off guard. I was shocked by his next announcements. He had met someone. I asked him what happened to the woman in South Africa. Apparently that love affair had finished shortly after she came back. At this point I was confused. He had just finished making a good case for us to get back together and now he was telling me he had a new girlfriend. I expressed my confusion. He explained that he had invited me to meet with him so we could discuss reconciliation. As I wasn't interested, he wanted to move in with Jean. He accused me of being unfair by asking us to wait. The pride in his voice as he made the next statement shocked me to the core. "You are my first choice. I will always love you and I would like to come home. I am giving you first refusal."

The words first refusal screamed in my head. This grand offer was an insult. Was I a business deal? This last thoughtless gesture closed the door on any possibility of reconciliation. I picked up my purse, wished him well and left.

On the drive home, I am not sure whether I laughed or cried. The rejection definitely hurt, but I was relieved that it really was over and amused at his arrogance of having a back-up plan. I still had difficulty letting go. Until then there had always been a glimmer of hope to hang on to and, even though I did not want to try again, I felt a reluctance to let go. Caught up in the emotions of the afternoon, I had not stopped to consider the impact of the day's event on our amicable relationship. The 'separation honeymoon' was over.

The dynamics of our relationship changed as Jean influenced Rodney. She too was a heavy drinker—drunks love to drink with other drunks. She was divorced, but didn't have any children. Judging by the way she treated my children, it was a good thing. Threatened by both us, it resulted in some bizarre behaviour and Rodney began to pull away from his children. Eventually, she persuaded Rodney to return to the U.K. Jean's mission was accomplished. Rodney disappeared from his children's lives and so did the support payments.

10

The Tornado Hits

All my strength had to go into taking care of my children and there was no getting away from it. I was a single mom and a tornado was about to go through my life!

Alone, scared and completely overwhelmed I began the task of raising five children. I don't remember what I did or how I did it. I can only describe my feelings as cold, bland, perhaps a more fitting description would be, 'Nothing, I shut down.' Primal instinct took over, I was 'mother bear' protecting and caring for my young. In some ways, things didn't change because Rodney had never been involved with the everyday childcare and household duties. His responsibilities were to take care of the outside, snow clearing, gardening and pool maintenance. It was different with two people sharing the responsibility of raising children and running a home.

After 16 years as a content stay-at-home mom, I now had a job outside the home. I completed the real estate course and became a licensed agent. The position met my need for flexibility and I was able to work from home but it was far more difficult to close sales and actually earn money than I ever expected. Fortunately, Rodney was still supporting us financially. Aware of being shy and timid, I had not realized I was an introvert and suffering from low self-esteem, I was my own worst enemy and found the real estate business difficult.

The 'hot shot' agents intimidated me and when I had clients, I was too shy to ask for the sale. I remember my first sale as if it was yesterday. I put my heart and soul into finding this nice young couple their dream home and I found it. They were very excited and wanted to put an offer in to buy the house. I can laugh at myself now, but at the time I thought, 'Oh my goodness, they want to buy the house, what do I do now?' My reply was "Are you sure?" I almost talked them out of buying their dream home. In spite of my shortcomings, I survived close to four years earning a modest income.

Rodney sold the cottage in Quebec and he and Jean bought a house in the city. He could never find time for the children and the support payments were erratic. He was pleading poverty and a change in circumstances; he was now supporting a common-law wife. I foolishly agreed to lower monthly payments and he agreed to find more time for the children. Jean pretended to like the children but it was obvious she couldn't cope. On reflection, I can imagine having five children dumped on you every two weeks was rather daunting and it was not surprising Rodney's relationship with the children deteriorated.

Going through a divorce and being a single parent in the late 70s was an anomaly and I treasured my friendship with Carol. We were both trying to come to terms with estranged spouses and raising kids on our own. We frequently talked until the wee small hours of the morning trying to make sense of our lives. During one of these sessions, Carol suggested I try some psychotherapy sessions since they were helping her. Therapy was a good decision. I found a psychologist and the therapy sessions were helpful. I was beginning to 'feel' again. I began to understand Rodney's drinking was not my fault and there was nothing I could do to stop it. I learned that I didn't have to be perfect and, most important of all, my confidence and self-esteem improved—enough for me to face the world without shame. An aptitude test confirmed my interest in marketing and I had enough confidence to register in the Marketing Certificate Program at the community college. It would take sometime to qualify as I had to attend night classes, but it was a start. I looked forward to returning to school in the fall.

Summer was approaching and I wanted a change in pace. Everyday life was a whirlwind and it seemed to get busier and more complex. The whirlwind was developing into a storm and it would not be long before I was spinning through a tornado. There was so much to do in a day. Schooling was a challenge. The children had learning disabilities and this was before mainstream schools could treat or even recognize the problems these gifted children faced. Luckily, through Rodney's connections at the university, we found a school that was experienced and equipped to teach these children. However, homework and transportation to and from school required more of my time.

Katrina was in Girl Guides and swam on the synchronized swim team. The older boys were swimmers too, and they swam for the local swim team. William was an active in Boy Scouts, James and Alex had joined Beavers. Add to this the daily household chores, my real estate job meeting clients and selling houses, attending school meetings, real estate meetings, I just never stopped. I coped by letting one day roll into the next without thinking too much.

Eventually I reached a breaking point, usually with a bad, snappy temper. It was time for a break. I explained to the children that Mum was in a bad mood and needed time for herself. My refuge was a hot bubble bath, a glass of wine and solitude. As I closed the bathroom door, my words were "I am only to be disturbed if someone is in imminent danger." This generally gave me about half an hour before there was a gentle tap on the bathroom door. The half hour was enough. I was re-energized and could face the rest of the day.

I can only remember one occasion when I was very close to 'losing it.'

I was upstairs vacuuming when I heard an extremely loud commotion downstairs. I turned off the machine and heard deathly silence followed by whispers, "Who is going to tell Mom?" "It wasn't my fault, it was yours…" and so the whispers continued. I crept downstairs, not knowing what to expect and I found three young boys sheepishly standing silently in front of the kitchen table. William, the eldest of the three, was the spokesman. Holding the broom in one hand and fidgeting he said, "Please don't be mad Mom, we didn't mean to break it." I asked them to move away from my new glass-topped kitchen table. As they slowly moved, I could see the glass was broken from one end of the table to the other. I was so mad, I thought I would burst. I turned around, went upstairs and I dared not even speak. Their story was that they were fighting over the broom—the reason for wanting the broom was never explained—and as one pulled, the other let go and the handle whacked against the table. William has since told me that they were not only scared because of the broken table but because they had never seen me so angry. Many weeks of forfeited allowance paid for the glass. I felt bad that I had scared them.

I was committed to providing my family with as 'normal' a life as possible, which often resulted in some funny episodes and our 'normal' vacation was one of them.

Camping and the outdoor life as you know was not my thing. Carol shared my view and what misguided whim ever put a camping vacation in our minds is a mystery to both of us. We decided that normal families took vacations and we should have a vacation. All we could afford was a piece of land to pitch a tent, so that was our explanation for camping.

As soon as school was out in late June, we packed up and headed for Calabogie Park. Two adults, seven kids and an incredible amount of camping gear—mostly borrowed—meant we had to take two cars. Calabogie Park was only a two-hour drive away. With its nice campsites, lakeshore and beach, safe swimming, a tuck-shop and communal games room, what more could we ask?

We hadn't even passed the city limits before I got lost. We stopped at McDonald's on the way out of town and I took the wrong turn getting back on the highway and arrived at the campsite an hour after Carol.

Our equipment included three tents: a large, full size tent for the four little ones, Alex, James, Jake and Sara, with Katrina old enough to keep an eye on the younger ones. Nathan and William had a pup tent. Carol and I shared a two-man tent. The large tent would double up for dining or activities if the weather turned wet. We pitched our tents, ate supper, the older kids went off to the games room and the little ones went to bed. Carol and I poured ourselves a glass of wine and sat by the campfire. It was a perfect moonlit night; stars twinkled between the branches of the pine trees and we could hear the water flap against the lakeshore. "Aha! This was the life."

Sleep came easily to us that night, a combination of fresh air and setting up camp knocked us all out. The call of the blue jay and the bright morning sun woke the children early, too early for us, so while the children played, we sipped coffee and tried to wake up before cooking a hearty breakfast of bacon, sausage and eggs. We spent a glorious day at the beach. The children swam and we soaked up the sun. By evening everyone was pretty tired and the kids turned in early. Carol and I sat at the picnic table watching the sky turn amazing shades of pink and coral as the sun set and dusk turned to night. There was no moon that night and the sky had clouded over, making it dark. I lit the gas lantern so we could see but it made everywhere else look even darker.

We heard twigs snapping and leaves rustling, as little creatures scurried about in the brush. The sounds were getting louder and seemed to be coming toward us. The snapping twigs sounded more like large cracking branches, and the bushes now rustled in a slow rhythmic way as though something or someone was approaching. I held my breath, looked at Carol and whispered as calmly as I could, "I think it's a bear."

We both jumped up and headed for my station wagon. Once in the car we closed the doors tightly and waited, but nothing appeared. I started to look around and to my horror, I realized I had left the tailgate of my station wagon wide open with food coolers stacked in the back—an invitation for the bear to join us—I muffled a screamed and as I did so a shadow moved into the clearing of the campsite. Terrified, my heart felt as though it would pound right out of my chest. The light from the lantern on the picnic table picked up the outline of the creature as he wandered into the clearing. The bear was smaller than I expected and on closer inspection it was a friendly cocker spaniel. Carol and I laughed so hard we frightened the poor dog away and almost woke the children.

We settled in for the night just as the rain started. The gentle patter on the tent was soothing and pleasant for a while, until the thunder boomed overhead and the lightening lit up the sky like a fireworks display. Thunderstorms make me feel vulnerable, especially when there is only a thin piece of canvas between me and Mother Nature in a really bad mood.

Sleep did not come easily to us that night. Surprisingly, the children slept through it and woke at the crack of dawn. The thunder continued to rumble and it rained off and on all that day as the storms rolled around the lake. The kids kept busy with games and swimming between the showers and we survived the day. Little Sara was complaining she was itchy, Carol rinsed her down in the lake and rubbed some cream on her, but then all the kids complained of being itchy and when we took a closer look, they all had a rash. Our immediate thought was an infectious disease, measles, chicken pox or something obscure we'd never heard of. It turns out the kids had 'swimmer's itch' caused by snail larvae that are found in the lake at certain times of the year and we managed to go camping at that exact time. We covered everyone with chamomile lotion and tried to settle for the night. I don't think any of us slept. Between itchy kids, wet sleeping bags and rain pouring into every corner of the tents, this was no longer fun. The next morning we packed up seven itchy, cranky kids, soggy wet tents and dripping sleeping bags and headed home for hot showers and comfy beds. That was the last time I ever went camping but we have laughed about our camping experience many times since.

11

Life's Twisting Tornado

By the end of the summer, the whirlwind was well on its way to turning into a full-blown twister. My life was spinning out of control. Any mother, single or not, will tell you there is more to do in a day than the day has hours. Every task has to be dealt with whether it is homework, cooking, nursing a sick child or dealing with a mini or major crisis. There is no such thing as 'not enough time.' You find the time and somehow make 36 hours of activities squeeze into 24. One disadvantage of being a single mom is there is no partner to pick up the slack. Not only do you squeeze more hours into a day, but you have to be in two places at once, sometimes three, like cooking supper and picking the kids up from swimming or meeting clients and attending a PTA meeting the same night.

My mother always used to say, "A problem shared is a problem halved," and that is true. When you are trying to handle problems and make decisions it helps to have two people to share the work and responsibility. There were many times when I felt the need for another opinion or the support of a partner, but there were also times when parenting alone had its advantages and actually made it easier. The children could not play one parent against the other. Making the decisions and setting the rules may have been more difficult, but once it was done, my word was gospel and there was no other opinion to consider. The children certainly made their opinions known and slammed doors and stomped around saying it wasn't fair, but there was nowhere for them to go so I think being a single mom had some advantages. I should mention that I was not a strict disciplinarian. I was a soft touch most of the time. The children knew this and managed to get away with quite a lot so one or two parents may not have made much difference on this score.

Blackburn Hamlet was a great neighbourhood for the children, but I needed to simplify my life. I moved from the suburbs to the city where there were activities for the children within walking distance and a good bus service. The old saying, 'Things have to get worse before they get better,' is very appropriate here.

My twisting life was already rotating out of control and now I had a move to handle. There was the house and much of the contents to sell (we were moving to a smaller place), clearing out the junk we had collected over twelve years, and the move itself. I had the sense to hire a moving company. Later that night, after they had moved the furniture into the new house, I returned to Blackburn Hamlet to finish cleaning and pick up the last few things, which included one of the cats that had escaped during the confusion. I was beyond exhausted but thank heaven for great friends who had rallied to help finish the cleaning.

My last task was to find Eric the cat. It was now one o'clock in the morning. The car was loaded with the last things and the front door was closed. "Where was that cat?" Eric, a fluffy orange and white male cat, had been neutered but maintained the male characteristics and liked to prowl at night and frankly he could be anywhere in the hamlet. I sat in the car and waited. He appeared about 15 minutes later. I tempted him with treats and finally got him in the car. Most cats hate cars, but Eric was terrified. It was a challenge for me to get into the car without letting Eric escape. At last we were in and Eric hid under the passenger seat, meowing mournfully.

As I drove away, a wave of sadness came over me. I was leaving the house of my dreams. My expectations were shattered and I had no idea what was in store for me. I started to cry, my sobs and cries were louder than the cat's. Utter despair poured from me, a sadness that I have only felt twice in my life. Whether or not it was my wailing that prompted Eric to come out from under the seat or he was just being brave I don't know, but he climbed onto the seat, meowing loudly. He roamed around the car for a while and finally settled on the headrest behind my head. This was fine at first until he became nervous and needed support and stood on my head. Every time the car moved, his claws came out to get a firm grip of scalp. As I was driving down Industrial Avenue, I noticed a police car off to the side of the road. Panic struck me and I said to the cat, "If this cop sees us he will pull me over." By now it was about two o'clock in the morning. Can you imagine what I looked like?

A tired, exhausted weeping young woman with a distraught yowling cat sitting on her head. There could not possibly be any sane explanation for this picture. And… if the cop stopped me, I would have no choice but to wind down my window and without a doubt the cat would be gone. So, I prayed, "Please God don't let the cop stop me." I was lucky that night. The police officer didn't stop me. He probably thought he was seeing things. My tears dried up and Eric chose a safer place to yowl. I began to laugh, now tears of laughter were streaming down my face. It was such a ridiculous picture.

Our new home was within biking distance of Rodney's house. I thought that if the kids could bike over to Rodney's for short visits, one or two kids at a time it would be easier for Jean. I was hopeful that the children would be able to establish a meaningful relationship with their father; but this was not to be.

Shortly after we moved, Rodney asked to meet with me and I agreed to meet on neutral ground. I was still nervous in Rodney's presence, although on this occasion I was more nervous about what he might have to say. We met at a local restaurant and talked over a meal. The conversation was civil and friendly. I even detected the same gentle concern in his voice that I heard on that fateful day, the day he came home to say he was leaving me. I was on high alert and with good reason. Rodney announced that he and Jean were moving to England. The house was up for sale. He had quit his job and planned to take a year off to look for a new family practice in England. Once again, the man had taken me by surprise and I was speechless. He did all he talking. He promised he would look after the kids and he would make sure I had enough money. He would give me several months in advance to cover me until he found a practice and would send monthly payments as soon as he was paid. The kids could come and visit during the school holidays as soon as he and Jean had a place to live.

Less than a month later, Rodney and Jean flew to England and completely abandoned the children, along with most of the support payments. Contact with Rodney after he arrived in England was limited to an occasional phone call for the kids. Except for the first Christmas, he couldn't even be bothered to remember birthdays or holidays. The kids said nothing but it must have hurt them. I was careful of what I said about Rodney in front of the children. I had this misguided idea that I should not speak ill of their father and I wanted the lines of communication to stay open for them.

I was on my own, breaking myself into little pieces. I felt fragmented, trying to care for the children, find enough love, enough time, enough energy and now, enough money to go around. I could no longer rely on regular payments from Rodney. Even my job was getting tougher. The tornado was picking up speed and I was being sucked into the funnel a little further each day.

Real estate was not bringing in enough money. I needed to find a job with a regular paycheque. I was doing well in my marketing studies, especially in the area of advertising so it wasn't surprising that advertising appealed to me. They hired me as an advertising representative for a well-known agency. Finally, I was doing something that I really liked and earning enough to support us—or so I thought. Sadly, the earnings turned out to be minimal and the company went bankrupt less than five months after I joined. So it was back to the drawing board. Fortunately, I had built up some good customer relationships during my time in advertising and one of my customers offered me a job selling telephone systems to small businesses. Remuneration was commissions only again, but beggars cannot be choosers. This time it paid off because I was promoted to customer service manager, a salaried position. I raised five children on $13,500 per year. Although this was a meagre salary even in 1983, it seemed like a fortune to me.

The task of raising my family was enormous and if I had stopped to think about it, I doubt I could have done it. I had no time to think or feel. I didn't want to because the only things I could feel were guilt, shame, hurt and pain. So the faster I spun in the tornado, the less I felt, and the less I felt, the easier it was to get on with life and give all I had to my children.

I wish I could say I found a magic solution that made everything better and helped me get through those years, but I did not. All I remember is repeating to myself, 'You can do this, you can get through this, just keep going one day at a time.' I kept going, I got through it, but I paid a personal price. I came through it physically, emotionally and financially exhausted.

For the most part, I allowed things to happen. I made very few deliberate choices, partly because I didn't have the energy to figure things out and partly because I didn't know how or what to do. Maybe my subconscious was making the decisions or perhaps the universe was guiding me and the things that happened were meant to happen.

It wasn't possible to do what I did without making some good choices. However, I can't help thinking that if I had made some different choices and taken more time to explore other opportunities, the outcome for me might have been better.

After we moved to the city, and knowing that Rodney was gone for good, I was back on my mission to provide my family with a 'normal' life. The kids should not miss out just because their father walked out on them. The Country Tennis Club was only two blocks from our house so I joined this prestigious club. I enjoyed playing tennis and had played with my father as a kid and teenager. I would teach my children the game of tennis.

The first time we went to play, all the courts were booked, so we went to the practice area. We were all dressed in our proper 'whites' and I was trying to look confident as I demonstrated to the children how to serve. Holding two balls in my hand I threw one ball in the air and as I swung my racket, the second ball fell to the ground and I did a kind of—not so graceful—pirouette on top of the ball and fell flat on my face. A very gallant gentleman came running over to help me and was eager to relieve my embarrassment by explaining how uneven the ground was at the point where I had fallen. I replied in all seriousness, "Oh no, I stood on the ball." The tennis club was a flop. The members were all affluent couples who had no time for a single mom with five kids. I didn't make any friends and the kids had no interest in tennis. The story of mom's pirouette on a tennis ball has created much laughter during family dinners.

The children were growing up and starting to develop their own interests and I wasn't always part of their lives. I had a house full of teenagers who knew it all and it was getting harder to keep tabs on them.

12

Katrina's Turbulent Teens

Stormy years without a father took its greatest toll on Katrina, my only daughter and the second eldest. You would think she would be a tomboy with four brothers but she was quite the opposite. Tiny and feminine, she loved frilly dresses, Barbie dolls and being a little mother to her younger brothers. Far from being subservient to her brothers, Katrina often ruled the roost. She and Nathan were great friends and the younger siblings looked up to her. Katrina's strong personality brushed up against Rodney constantly, so now that he was out of the picture, life would be much easier for her, or so I thought.

Growing up through those teenage years is hard for all children and even harder without a father. What I was not aware of was that it is especially difficult for daughters, as they desperately need their father's approval to move out into the world. Communication with Rodney was nonexistent. Not only was he on the other side of the Atlantic Ocean, but he made no attempt to phone or write, even at Christmas or on birthdays. Missing her father, Katrina searched for fatherly approval in all the wrong places.

My cute little girl had a mature, sensible mind of her own. She always rose above the pack and would never be coerced into following either fads or fashions. I worried about her being a goody two shoes, a 'Sandra Dee' character (from the movie Grease) and not fitting in with the high school crowd. That was until the day she joined the pack and moved away from me. Every parent, mother, father, single or married knows that sickening, helpless feeling as you watch as your child walk the wrong path and know there is nothing you do can do to stop it.

Katrina's best friend Jillian lived on the same street and they had been best friends through grade school and now in high school, they were inseparable. It was not unusual for them to go out together but on this occasion my instinct was telling me something was wrong. That morning I came across Katrina's diary. I knew I was invading her privacy but with just cause. The diary told me more than I wanted to know. They were meeting with boys much older than themselves and they had lied about where they were going. Thinking I was doing the responsible and neighbourly thing, I went to see Jillian's mother and told her what I knew. This was a big mistake. I was told that Jillian would never lie nor would she do anything wrong. Katrina was the bad influence. Without a father, there was not enough love in the family. What else could she expect? I left their house feeling battered and bruised from the tongue-lashing. Still worried about the girls, I was proactive, got in the car and looked for them. Based on Katrina's diary and a little detective work, I had a rough idea where to look. I found them and brought them home. Jillian did tell her parents the truth but her mother never spoke to me again. It amazed me how many parents, particularly those in suburbia with the 'big hats,' would ignore warning signs and pretend their kids could do no wrong.

Punk rock was the fad in the '80s and this was Katrina's way of rebelling. And rebel she did. I was never sure if she would survive and I had grave doubts that I would.

However, in the midst of incredible tension, there were some funny episodes and thankfully I could still laugh. On this particular Saturday night my friend and I were sitting at the dining room table playing Scrabble when Katrina came bouncing into the house yelling that she had brought Jimmy home to meet me. Pondering my next move and studying the letter tiles I said, "Pleased to…" I stopped mid-sentence as I lifted my head and saw Jimmy. Well, actually the first thing I saw was a bright orange Mohawk hairdo that rose from the top of this five foot nothing, scrawny kid with a large safety pin piercing each ear. I tried to lower my shocked eyebrows and lift my cheeks into a smile as I finish my sentence, "… meet you, Jimmy."

Jimmy was a harmless character; just a mixed-up teenager like Katrina. But they were running with an undesirable crowd who I suspected were involved with drugs and petty crime. My concerns were confirmed when I was called into the vice-principal's office at Katrina's school. Miss Radcliffe expressed concern about Katrina as she was on the fringe of a terrible crowd of kids and could either join this bad group or move away from them. She said that because Katrina came from a 'broken home,' she did not think there was enough love at home to keep her from falling in with this crowd. I informed Miss Radcliffe, in no uncertain terms, that there was as much love and possibly more love in our 'broken home' as in any 'normal' home. This interview upset me. Firstly, because she implied I did not love my daughter, secondly because she was confirming my own concerns and thirdly, although her comments were well meant, she offered no advice to help solve the problem.

Curfews and punishments just didn't work. If I told Katrina to be home by eleven o'clock she rolled in at two or three in the morning. But she did come home. We had shouting matches and arguments that would curl your hair. Always the same topics. Her coming home in the middle of the night. Who she was with? What was she doing? How could she go out looking like that? I remember watching her walk up our street one day dressed in a short black skirt that hardly covered her bum, black fishnet stockings, high-heeled shoes she couldn't walk in and a tight black tee shirt. Her makeup was almost white with thick black lines drawn around her eyes—raccoon style—purple lipstick and raven black hair. I wasn't sure whether to describe her as a hooker or Lily Munster (from the TV show The Munsters). In spite of the way she looked, I knew I loved her very much and something inside me told me to love her unconditionally and always leave the door open.

Our constant arguing and fighting was disrupting the family. The boys would leave the room or even the house when we started and goodness knows what the neighbours thought as we screamed at each other. Something had to be done.

Somehow we had to learn to get along with each other or I was going to lose my daughter and I wasn't about to let that happen. I received mixed advice. Some people suggested I throw her out because she was too disruptive. I needed to think of the other children. One psychologist suggested, 'tough love.' He explained how important my love was to Katrina. The objective of 'tough love' was to modify the child's behaviour. If the child followed the rules, you showered them with love. If their behaviour was unacceptable, you withdrew your love. Neither of these options were acceptable to me. In my opinion, Katrina needed lots of unconditional love and she needed to know I was always there for her.

I had difficulty understanding how throwing a 15-year-old who was already in crisis out on the street was going to help either of us. The bottom line was I could not and would not either withhold my love or throw her out. Thankfully, I followed my own instincts. I started to listen instead of yelling and I tried understanding instead of judging. I continued to set limits, which were rarely adhered too, but they were there. Although I did not approve of most of her friends, I was confident that Katrina's strong mind would keep her on the straight and narrow (albeit shakily at times). I kept most of my opinions to myself and tried to be supportive. The cat fights calmed and we could talk to each other and I persuaded her to see a therapist. I told her constantly how much I loved her and she knew I would always be there for her no matter what happened.

In spite of therapy, which seemed to help, Katrina left home. She had this romantic notion that living on student welfare with Jimmy and a bunch of friends was a 'cool' thing to do. I tried to persuade her not to go but she was stubborn and determined. I reluctantly gave her my blessing and helped her move her stuff. The house was an old, rundown row house in the centre of town, situated in a very poor neighbourhood frequented by hookers and drug dealers. Miss Radcliffe's words began to haunt me. I was terrified and beside myself with worry, fearing the worst for my sweet little girl's safety. Katrina, like most teenagers, frequently accused me of not understanding and on this occasion, I truly did not understand. Many of you reading this are saying, "How could you let her go?" If I thought it would work, I would have tied her to the bed and locked her in the house. I would have done anything to stop her but I understood my daughter. I knew I could not force her to stay home. Even if I tried, she would run away and then I would lose her forever. At least this way, the lines of communication stayed open and she kept in touch with home. It was a life line, admittedly a very thin thread, but it was strong enough to survive.

Less than a month after the big move, Katrina phoned in tears. My heart missed a beat and I was scared. Between the sobs she said, "Mom the whole ceiling just fell on top of us and the landlord has refused to even look at it. He says we have to move out. Can I come home and how soon can you pick me up?" I breathed a sigh of relief and brought her home. I thanked God for guiding me to follow my own instincts and for keeping her safe.

There were many turbulent years as Katrina developed her free spirit.

She and the boyfriend moved to Toronto when she was only sixteen. She got a good job in Toronto's financial district as a runner and did well. They lived in a horrible apartment with cockroaches, rats in the alley and Portuguese families who screamed at each in the middle of the night—my experience from one visit. Katrina grew up and found herself. After several years in Toronto, she moved back to Ottawa and from then on we became best friends and soul mates. Many, many years later, she settled down and has a family of her own. There is still a rebel inside her, a charming rebel that I am proud of.

Every relationship is different and every person sees the world in a different way, but my advice to a parent raising a difficult teenager is to love them unconditionally, no matter what. Set limits. As an adult, Katrina tells me that setting curfews and limits worked. Although she rarely came home on time, because of the limits she came home. She never acknowledged my love during those turbulent years and I was never sure if she understood how much I loved her. Now Katrina tells me that she always knew how much I loved her and knowing that she could always come home gave her enough security to grow up, stick to her own principles and in spite of the odds, stay away from crime and drugs. She did not fall in with the wrong crowd and there was enough love in our home, 'broken' or not.

13

Teenage Boys

Teenage boys were a whole different story. The boys didn't rebel in the same way. They played loud music, dressed in anything black and grew their hair long and bushy. The boys had curly hair, so as it grew it looked like an afro haircut. They seemed to think it was cool to use as many swear words as possible in a sentence that always finished with the word 'man.' I am very aware of how sexist this may sound, but I did not worry about the boys in the same way as I worried about Katrina. I always felt they could defend themselves better, so although the same curfews and the rules applied to everyone, I was more lenient with the boys. They missed having a father around but rarely said anything. Each of them found a 'father' figure who helped them grow up, and they looked to one another for support and advice. It wasn't cool for boys to admit they discussed their thoughts and activities with their mother. I was lucky because I think they talked to me quite a lot. I was only told what they wanted me to hear, but moms have a way of knowing a great deal more than their offspring realize.

It is wise for parents of teenagers to choose their battles carefully. Some things just are not worth fighting over. Children, especially teenagers, need guidance, not ridicule. I have always been a firm believer that we all earn respect and how can we expect children—of any age—to have respect for us if we do not show them respect. I'll never forget the day I asked Nathan some very intrusive questions regarding his recent break-up with his girlfriend. He very quietly said, "Mom this is none of your business." Once I got over the shock, I realized he was right and it was time for me to respect his privacy. On another occasion when he was much younger, maybe fourteen, I lost my temper. It was one of those days when everything accumulates, a bad day at work, the car broke down, there was a fight with Katrina and suddenly I snapped. Nathan was the closest and I lashed out at him. But as I did, I looked up at this six-foot kid with fire in his eyes and realized two things: he had done nothing to deserve my outburst and he was much bigger than me. It was time to show this young adult more respect.

We had hardly any money, so the children were expected to get part-time jobs as soon as they were able. Between school, homework and jobs they didn't have much time to get into trouble. Curfews and rules didn't seem to be a problem with the boys. I was very proud of the fact that all my children had a very good work ethic, which I am sure stemmed from being raised on very little and learning if they wanted something, they had to work for it. Money did not grow on trees in our house. Nathan had lots of friends. I knew most of them as they had grown up together and I was—and still am—known as Mom number two to Dave, his best friend, so I knew where he was with most of the time.

I do remember the shock of looking at my seventeen-year-old son with his head shaved as clean as a baby's bottom. The friends that I thought I knew so well had dared him to do it. I was so upset I made him wear a hat at the dinner table. Why I was so upset, I am not sure. It seems so trivial now, but back in the 80s, people didn't shave their heads like they do today. The difficulty I had with Nathan was trying to keep him in school and, when it became clear he would not finish, I suggested he visit his father. He was fourteen when Rodney left, enough time to bond and he had always been close to his dad. We used to laugh when they walked down the street together since they had the same walk and mannerisms. Nathan needed his father, so I bought him an open return ticket to England, which was good for a year. He could come home any time, but perhaps living with his dad would help him grow up and decide what he wanted to do with his life. Now why I would think that a man who had abandoned his children would want to be a father to his teenage son is a mystery to me, but I wanted Nathan to get to know his dad so I sent him off to England.

Rodney lived on the south coast of England in a small seaside town and there was very little work. Nathan saw an opportunity to set up a small business selling ice cream to the tourists and he did well during the summer. But as the sunshine vanished, the tourists went home and winter set in and nobody wanted ice cream. Poor Nathan was out of work. Rodney told him to leave because there was no work for him and they couldn't—or wouldn't—support him. To this day, I have difficulty believing that Rodney could be so callous to his son. Nathan left and went up north to his aunt, Rodney's sister, a lovely lady who made him welcome.

It was close to Christmas when I found out Rodney had thrown his son out of the house and I was furious. I couldn't comprehend how a father could do it, especially just before Christmas. I wasn't sure how long he would stay at Mary's and I worried that Nathan would be alone for the holidays.

Christmas was always a big holiday in our house so I called my parents who offered to go pick him up for Christmas. Nathan was very fond of his Aunt Mary and he wanted to spend Christmas with her. She was not at all like her brother and was on her own and very proud of her nephew. Nathan did go to his grandparents for New Year's and after some long talks with his grandfather—the mentor he needed so badly—he came home to Canada. He never finished high school, but by using his exceptional creative talents and knowing what he wanted, he worked his way up and became a successful film editor.

The opposite of Nathan, William, the middle boy, knew what he wanted out of life even before he left grade school. From the age of fourteen he planned his life to become an engineer and that was all he thought about. He had neither time nor inclination to rebel. I remember him shaking his head at some of the antics of his siblings and friends. Our friends, Mary and Colin, stood by the family after Rodney left. Their son John was Williams's best friend. In fact they were so close that when we moved away from Blackburn Hamlet, they found John sleepwalking over to our old house looking for William. Colin treated William like a son and William looked up to Colin. The positive influence that family had on William was second to none. I am convinced that William's positive outlook on life and his determination to follow his own path, came from Colin.

By the time Alex and James reached their teenage years, I was getting pretty street smart, or so I thought. They had their older siblings to look up to, talk to and cover up for them. I remember our neighbour, Bill Holt, alerting me to the fact that Alex had a fiery temper and would come to no good because he didn't have a father to discipline him. I found this odd as this same neighbour told me what a wonderful kid James was and how he would do well. Bill's son Mike was James' closest friend so this may have made the difference. The Holts were a musical family and James was musically talented. The Holt family had a great influence on James and I am thankful for the support and encouragement they gave him.

Both Alex and James either didn't get into too much trouble or they kept it from me and I think it was the latter. I do remember suspecting Alex and his friends were experimenting with alcohol. The kids liked to hang out at the 7-Eleven store drinking Coca-Colas or 'Slurpys,' which were harmless, but I was not so sure that was all they were drinking. One day I asked Alex if he had been drinking. He looked surprised at my question and denied it. I persisted with more questions until Alex finally admitted that a bunch of them had walked down to the park with sodas and one guy had a mickey of gin so they mixed it with the Coca-Cola. Yuck! I was thinking that gin and Coke-Cola would not make a very tasty combination. Alex told me it tasted good, but the expression on his face told me a different story. Alex began working part-time in a restaurant shortly after that so he didn't have time for anything else. James had a strong desire to become a musician and he played the double bass and practiced constantly with his friend Mike.

The transition from child to adult—the teenage years—are tough for both child and parent, whether you are a single parent or a traditional family and my stories are probably true of most families. My children had to battle the stigma of coming from a 'broken home.' It was an affliction that implied that my children were a bad influence, of what—we were never sure. I was second-guessing myself all the time because I decided on curfews and what was acceptable and what was not. The advantage of being a one parent family was that I had no one to question or disagree with me. I prided myself on being an 'open book' mom. I always had my eyes and ears open, as well as my mind. It was important to keep close to my children and keep a balance between knowing what was going on and being too intrusive.

14

Dancing in the Rain

While the storm was raging, I was dancing in the rain trying to 'find myself.' At first I was too busy, scared and shy to look for new friends or to socialize outside work and home. It was perhaps true to say that new friends found me. Old friends treated me differently. I was no longer part of a couple and I didn't fit in with the group anymore. Strangers became new friends but the singles scene was very foreign to me. In spite of my reluctance, a well meaning, and newly single, friend dragged me screaming and kicking to disco bars (late 70s, early 80s) and even on a couple of blind dates. We had a blast! It had been almost twenty years since I had socialized without a partner and the only way I knew how to behave was to be eighteen again. My naiveté led me into some funny and dangerous situations and I am eternally grateful to streetwise friends for coming to my rescue on more than one occasion.

Gossip travels fast in a place like Blackburn Hamlet, so once the news broke that Rodney had moved out, my status in the community changed. I am not sure if I pulled away from them or they pulled away from me but I was definitely living in a different world. Carol lived in the same community and I was to meet one other divorced single mom from the area. I had met Martha briefly and, when the news of my separation reached her ears, she called me immediately. It was comforting to talk to someone else who had been through a separation. Martha insisted that I needed to get out, have some fun and meet men, lots of them. Going out and having fun sounded like a good idea, but meeting men, even 'dating?' I was not so enthusiastic about that.

Martha was an outgoing, gregarious person, the extreme opposite of me, and Carol's personality was somewhere in the middle. Circumstances pulled us together as friends and, on occasions, we were referred to as the three musketeers. On reflection, I don't think it was an accurate description but it was Martha's interpretation. I was certainly a friend to both, but they were very different types of friendship. Carol's was to become very close and long lasting, while Martha's, although I didn't realize it at the time, was superficial and neither reciprocated nor long term. However, for the few years that we teamed up as the three musketeers, we learned to socialize, enjoy ourselves and even date guys again.

Safety in numbers was our motto. We went out together and came home together. Disco was all the rage at the time and once a week we went to 'Sacha's,' a disco situated in the Four Season's Hotel in downtown Ottawa. We danced all night to Saturday Night Fever and the Bee Gees. The room was packed with people and very dark, making it difficult to move around. Loud music made conversation almost impossible so dancing was all you could do. The dance floor was raised about three feet and the only light came from the dance floor, brightly lit from under the floor and flashed in sync with the strobe lights from the ceiling above. We were never short of partners. The clientele was a mixture of local people and out-of-town businessmen, hence our reasoning for always going together and leaving together. We rarely gave out our phone numbers or pursued friendships from the disco, except for our own group of friends. When it was time to leave, we would say our goodbyes and thank our dance partners for a fun evening, while refusing a ride home from the locals or a nightcap from the out-of-towners. We were amused at the disappointment of these men as they nearly always had more than dancing on their mind. I am sure they were cursing us as the evening was coming to a close and there was little time to find a willing partner for the night.

Once in a while, we broke the rules and it was on one such occasion that Martha and I ran into trouble. I had been dancing with this guy all evening. What a dancer! He was such a nice person, good looking and money appeared to be no object as he bought me drinks and talked about his boat on the St. Lawrence River. He wasn't shy to tell me about himself. His name was Jason Smythe, he was vice-president of marketing for the Peek Frean Biscuit Company. He lived in Montreal and traveled all over the world on business. At the end of the evening, he asked for my phone number. I felt I really knew this guy and could trust him so I broke rule number one and gave him my number. He called to let me know he was coming to town the following week and wanted to take me out for dinner. He explained he was meeting a business associate and did I have a friend to make up a foursome? Great idea, I thought. I would ask Martha to join us.

Martha, a bit worldlier than I, questioned this man's motives. I assured her he was okay and we could trust him. As long as we stuck together, we would be all right. I was so excited. It had been years since I had 'gone on a date' and this was no ordinary date. We were going to the Château Hotel for dinner and dancing in semi-formal attire. I bought myself the most gorgeous black velvet pantsuit and I looked stunning. Martha and I kept to our rules by insisting we would drive ourselves to the hotel and meet them in the lobby.

I felt like a million dollars as I walked into the ballroom on this man's arm. Dinner was wonderful. We took our time and danced to a live orchestra between courses. It was very romantic and we enjoyed each other's company. After dinner the guys invited us to their suite for a drink and we broke rule number two by accepting the invitation.

The suite was set up as a hospitality room with a large display of products on the table, mostly cameras and electronic equipment and not a biscuit in sight. I said, "Jason, I thought you worked for Peek Frean." He replied, "Oh no, whatever gave you that idea? I'm district sales manager for Cam Cameras and I'm here for a trade show." At this point, I was feeling uncomfortable. I knew he told me he worked for Peek Frean. I glanced across to Martha, who looked at the table and gave me a quizzical look. I shrugged my shoulders and she made some gestures toward the door. I stupidly shook my head, not understanding what she was trying to tell me. I took the drink he just poured for me and sat on the couch. Martha didn't drink so she asked for a glass of water. While Jason went to get the water, she once again gestured toward the door. I took a sip of my drink and almost choked on the amount of alcohol it contained. Only then did I realize what Martha was trying to tell me. These guys were not who they appeared to be and we needed to get out of there.

I looked at my watch and said, "Oh, is that the time? We have to leave now. I have to be home for my babysitter." Jason laughed and replied, "The night is young, my dear. We have lots of fun in store for both of you." Martha had the sense not to sit down and was trying to move toward the door. I tried to get up from the couch but Jason pushed me down and his arms come around me like an octopus. His hands were everywhere. I tried to get up again and screamed at him, "Leave me alone!" Jason got angry and cursed and called us "bitches and prick teasers." I stood up and asked, "Whatever gave you the idea we were going to sleep with you?" Jason yelled, "Why do you think I spent all that money on dinner tonight? You owe me." With that, he grabbed my arms and started to drag me toward the bedroom. I was now screaming and crying and frightened out of my mind. Martha picked up the phone and, as she dialed the front desk, she called out to him, "Let her go or I will call the police!" The front desk had answered and was asking if everything was okay.

Jason let me go and we ran for the door. As we raced down the hall, Jason was still yelling but he didn't follow us. When the elevator door opened at the lobby, the front desk clerk was waiting for us and was prepared to call the police. We didn't think that was necessary and were happy just to have escaped unharmed. I learned a valuable lesson that night about trusting and being street smart. If it hadn't been for Martha's intuition and quick thinking, there is no doubt in my mind that I would have been raped. Thank you, Martha, wherever you are.

Trying to find a place to meet that wasn't a 'meat market' with an average age of twenty- something was a challenge. There is a difference between being single looking for a mate and single-divorced-and-comes-with-five-kids. My idea of going to a bar was not to be picked up by some guy but to talk and enjoy some adult company.

A group of us established a routine of meeting at Christopher's Pub every Friday night after work for a couple of hours to have a drink and talk about our week before heading home. Occasionally we went out for supper or to a movie and nearly always as a group. Martha was the life and soul of the group. Always organizing parties and fun things, she was a real party animal. She didn't drink or smoke, but she loved a good time. Her only vice was men, and she had plenty of them at her beck and call. They just flocked around her and she flirted mercilessly. I remember one Friday evening at Christopher's Pub, she was being so flirtatious that it embarrassed me. I finally spoke up. "Martha if you don't stop flirting I am leaving!" I sounded so much like her mother that we all burst out laughing and she settled down. Her behaviour embarrassed me but I secretly loved being on the fringe of her gregarious personality.

That particular evening I met Chad. He fancied himself a great cook and invited Martha and I for dinner. Remembering our last escapade, I wasn't keen to go and risk a repeat of 'Mr. Peak Frean.' Martha assured me she had been out with Chad several times. He was a nice guy and a good cook. I trusted her judgment.

We arrived with a bottle of wine and some cookies. Martha doesn't drink but she bakes. Chad welcomed us and we joined him in the kitchen while he put the finishing touches to the meal. The aromas from the stove were wonderful, making us hungry for this fabulous smelling food. The table was perfect. Martha Stewart would have been proud of him. There were flowers in the centre, napkins and matching china. Why I always expect guys to eat off old, cracked mismatched plates, I don't know, but this table looked elegant. The meal started with shrimps in wine sauce followed by a French dish, Poulet Basque. The meal was delicious and we all ate too much. Chad told us he had a special dessert, but suggested we go into the living room and relax over coffee for a while. That sounded like a splendid idea. Half an hour later, Chad excused himself and disappeared for about 15 minutes.

We assumed he was making dessert and chatted between ourselves. Then we heard this sort of drum roll as Chad leapt into the living room with his arms and legs spread-eagled and shouted with great gusto "dessert is served." He stood in front of us as naked as the day he was born. We took one look at him and burst out laughing. Martha told him to go put his clothes back on since he looked ridiculous. He was determined to be dessert and insisted that we take off our clothes. He was looking forward to a ménage à trois. This was no longer funny as Chad got upset. I think our laughing hurt his ego and he was not going to get dressed. We made a dash for the door. Thankfully it was unlocked and we ran out into the hallway and, to our surprise he followed us, still naked with the 'family jewels' wafting in the breeze as he ran down the hall yelling, "We aren't finished. I cooked dinner and now I want dessert." We jumped into the elevator and half expected Chad to follow but he must have decided not to join us. We laughed until it hurt, tears streaming down our faces as we walked to the car. Grateful we had once again escaped unharmed, the picture of 'dessert is served' brought us back to peals of laughter.

15

Losses and Heartbreak

Martha was always on a date and sometimes dragged me along, usually to make up a foursome. It was on one such occasion that I met Lenny. Martha thought that I needed to date more. I still did not feel comfortable dating. With the help of her current boyfriend Ken, she set me up on a blind date with Ken's friend Lenny.

We met the guys at the restaurant. After supper, we went to one of the trendy bars. I was so paranoid that I insisted we drive from the restaurant to the bar in separate cars. The guys were a little perplexed at this plan, but they didn't comment and accepted our decision. We had a great evening. I really liked Lenny, tall and good looking. I like tall men. He was fun but not overwhelming and we had a nice date. When I didn't hear from him, I assumed he wasn't interested and brushed it off. Two weeks after the blind date, he called and invited me to a barbecue at his place. He barbecued steaks and we had a quiet evening listening to music and getting to know each other. That was the start of an adventure that lasted three years.

Everyone should have at least one passionate adventure in his or her life and my relationship with Lenny was very passionate. The chemistry between us was electric. I have never been loved by anyone nor have I loved so passionately before or since.

Lenny was an easy-going, fun-loving guy. Our relationship was an adventure because we did things I had never done before. I experienced a rock concert, when the Eagles appeared at the racetrack. I remember the incredibly long line up in the boiling summer sun. I had never seen so many people in one place. We found our seats. Lenny had insisted we have seats in the stand so we could see the stage. However the Eagles were so far away, they looked like ants. But that didn't matter. The hype, the atmosphere and the music created the whole concert experience. He enjoyed surprising me with romantic weekends, the best one being a winter getaway in Quebec. It was a winter wonderland. We walked in the snow, skated on the river, and gulped hot chocolate in front of an enormous log fire. I learned to enjoy baseball. We were great fans of the Montreal Expos back in the days when the 'Big O' was packed with fans. My children did not frighten Lenny. Most men ran as fast as they could when I told them I had five kids. Lenny enjoyed my children and would bring his son, Mark, to stay with us sometimes. Alex, William and Mark became good friends. Most of all, we just wanted to be together, our own paradise. It didn't matter whether we were alone, with the children or out with friends, the chemistry was always there.

Lenny placed me on a pedestal. He adored me. We held hands, touched and hugged each other constantly and oh those kisses, kisses that would often lead us to beautiful lovemaking. Lenny called me his 'lady.' He was proud of me and protective. He made it very clear to all his friends who I belonged to. I had never been treated in this way before. I adored him and was proud to be his 'lady.' By today's standards, this last paragraph sounds sexist, but it wasn't like that at all.

As wonderful and passionate as this relationship was, there was a dark side. Alcohol and drugs were to haunt me again. Lenny drank a great deal—it was nothing for him to drink a case of beer in an evening—but he never appeared to be drunk and was always in control. He never uttered an angry word and never, ever lifted a finger or threatened abuse of any kind. His happy and laid back disposition just became happier and more laid back, although this could have been because of his other vice, smoking marijuana. He smoked daily and it made me uncomfortable. I pleaded with him to give it up. It was illegal and I was afraid they would arrest him, but he saw nothing wrong with his habit and would not stop. I made him promise not to smoke in the house or near the children, or even express his liberal opinion regarding the marijuana laws in my home and he respected my request.

I never thought of our relationship as being long term. The thought of marrying or moving in together just did not enter my head. My children still came first and I would not subject them to a stepfather. My 'mother bear' instincts to protect my children were strong. I could not handle anyone other than myself criticizing or disciplining them, even with just cause.

I didn't want to admit that the marijuana issue was more than just smoking. It was part of a much bigger issue, one of personal values and morals. No matter how I looked at it or how I justified his opinion, it was clear that our value systems were different. For three years I struggled with my own conscience. I was torn between being true to myself and the love and passion I felt for this man, until the day he lied to me.

Some months earlier he had been involved in a car accident, nothing serious. Someone rear-ended him. It was not his fault, his car was fixed, end of story. Out of the blue he told me his lawyer has advised him to sue the guy who caused the accident and so he would be busy with lawyers and court appearances for the next little while. The story was feasible, but I had a nagging thought that something wasn't quite right. Lenny was on edge and definitely not his usual laid back self. He brushed it off as being tired and preoccupied with the court case.

During a phone conversation with Martha, she mentioned Lenny's upcoming court case, only it had nothing to do with an automobile accident. What a rude awakening!

Lenny had been arrested and charged with trafficking marijuana. His frequent visits to his lawyer were to prepare for his defense. To say I felt angry, hurt and betrayed was an understatement. Words could not describe how I felt. I didn't ask him for an explanation. I just finished the relationship right then and there. They say love is blind and I was certainly blinded. I felt guilty for allowing my love for him to mask my responsibilities. I went into a panic thinking of how I had exposed my kids to a criminal and the dangers that it might have brought. My imagination was getting the better of me and I became paranoid. I worried I was being followed or my phone tapped. An acquaintance in the police force suggested that I call the police department and ask if it implicated me. I didn't realize you could do that. The police were helpful and, although they could not talk about the case, they reassured me that I was not part of any investigation. Relieved at this news, I stopped looking over my shoulder.

The only time I wondered if our family's association with Lenny had an influence on us was when we traveled. I had never had a problem with customs but Katrina was searched and scrutinized for hours when she returned from a vacation in England. She was about 16 at the time so it could have been because of the association with her present circle of undesirable friends, her association with Lenny or maybe just an unlucky spot check. Customs found nothing but Katrina was shaken by the ordeal. Whatever the reason, this incident was a wake- up call. If my association with Lenny had something to do with my daughter being searched at customs, his drug habit had most certainly affected the family's integrity. I needed to learn to trust my own judgment.

I was sad and grieved for a long time. Although I had always known the relationship was never to be permanent, I missed him very much. I had no regrets about this passionate adventure that had passed through my life and I would never forget him. We met once again, about 12 years later. Our eyes met. He smiled and I could feel the warmth as we hugged each other. The chemistry just flowed between us and always would.

I completely lost my trust in men after my adventure with Lenny and I rarely dated except with known friends. Most of my socializing was with Carol and Martha. We were older and wiser and no longer needed to dance in the rain.

Maybe I was drowning my sorrows or perhaps I just needed to fill that empty space after I stopped seeing Lenny. Whatever the reason, I made a major career change. I had done well in the telecommunications business. I had worked my way up to Manager of Customer Service and Training. I liked what I was doing. But I reported directly to the General Manager and I discovered he was less than ethical. After he had involved me in some of his schemes of hiring people, making promises he couldn't keep and then firing them without cause, I finally quit in frustration, taking a similar position in another company. I discovered two weeks later that my former manager's contract had not been renewed. Had I known this, I would not have resigned. I knew the first day I walked into the new job, that I had made a mistake. I would have liked to go back but didn't have the courage to ask. I didn't stay in the telecommunications business after I switched jobs.

Instead I decided to be my own boss by opening a business. I went from high-tech telecommunications to low-tech cake decorating, rekindling my creativity and domestic science skills. The idea was to invest my meagre savings into the business and, in return, the business would provide us with a better standard of living and much needed money for the children's university or college education. Once the children left home, the profits from the business would become my retirement plan.

'Simply Elegant Cakes' was born. We made cakes for all occasions and the business took off. We became famous for our unique and customized products. We had some pretty weird requests including one bride who wanted her wedding cake to look like a green field with black and white Holstein cows grazing in it (she was marrying a farmer). We accommodated her request with sugar paste cows, fences and trees. The most difficult customer I encountered was an overly anxious mother of the bride, who wanted the wedding to be perfect. That wasn't unusual but her complaint was bizarre. She was furious because the green leaves decorating the wedding cake did not match the green in her new carpet. She demanded her money back. The most spectacular cake we ever made was for the architect who designed the Museum of Civilization. The cake was a replica of the museum, a magnificent piece of art.

The hours were long. I started at five in the morning and rarely finished until ten at night. This was the one time in my life that I felt I neglected my children. They were old enough to look after themselves but I didn't give them enough of my time. I was either working or attending to the essentials in the home. I lost sight of my priorities during the time I owned the bakery and I deeply regret those few years.

The initial success encouraged me to expand the business into a full bakery and, with some financial help from my mother and the bank, we moved to new premises. Expanding so quickly was a mistake. I had too much overhead. The location, although it seemed perfect, turned out to be bad for business. It was a new strip mall under construction with a large office building at the back, a ready client for my kind of business. Unfortunately, the completion was delayed several times and the office building backed out. I could have left as well but decided to stay, expecting another tenant would take over the build. The building stayed empty for a long time and I had not allowed enough contingency funding to cover the slow times. Burnt out and finding it difficult to promote the business effectively, I was overwhelmed. I was trying to be superwoman and do it all myself, since delegating was not one of my strong points. Simply Elegant Cakes, in spite of its success, was on the path to failure. I tried everything. I sought advice from friends and professionals and even sold my house to try to keep the business afloat, but to no avail. A year later, I put the business into receivership.

The grief and loss I felt from closing the business was overwhelming. If I hadn't lived it, I would never have believed the devastating effect it would have on me. I cried for weeks. I was humiliated and so ashamed. How could I face people? I was such a failure. There was no money left for the children's education. My home was gone. I had lost my mother's money and I had nothing for my retirement. I had no idea what I was going to do, other than pray.

My prayers were answered. When God closes one door, He opens a window and He opened a window for me. Sovereign Bakery Foods supplied my business with bakery ingredients and they just happened to be looking for a sales representative for Eastern Ontario. I was well qualified for the position and hired immediately. I couldn't believe my luck. The job paid well and for the first time since my divorce, I actually had enough money to raise my family. The benefits included paid vacation, sick leave, extended medical and a pension plan as well as a company car. I had hit the jackpot! The bonus was I loved the job and had a great boss. I could buy a house, thanks once again to my mother's help and a regular paycheque. I could help the children prepare for their adult lives and there was enough left over to start a retirement savings plan.

The tornado was subsiding. The children were almost all grown up and I could move on with my life—or could I?

16

The Tornado Subsides

Close to twenty years had passed since 'that fateful day.' James, the youngest, graduated from university. The other children were settling into their adult lives. It felt strange, like the uneasy calm after the storm. The adrenaline was still pumping through my veins. I was still on high alert but there was no one home to watch over. I was racing against time but there was plenty of time. The storm had calmed but I had not, and I felt uneasy. I wondered, 'What do I do now?'

The tornado left me battered and bruised, with little pieces of me scattered everywhere. My self-worth was defined by my role of mother and protector. My mind full of questions, my emotions depleted, my body tired and broken and my finances spent. Was there anything left for me? The children were busy with their own lives so it was time for me to step back from theirs and look to my own.

I have always had a lot of friends and it was the companionship and caring from them that helped to fill the void. Carol and I spent many hours talking and looking for answers. Therapists and friends suggested that we were suffering from the 'empty nest' syndrome. We searched the self-help section of the library and bookstores for books on this subject and between us we must have read them all. But nothing addressed the way we felt. Then I realized this was no empty nest, but a run down vacant building; nothing but a crumbling shell waiting for the wrecker's ball!

Hey, just a minute! Old buildings have character and personality. They deserve to be restored. Like a building, I could be refurbished and rebuilt both inside and out. It was time to develop my authentic self and view my scars as respectable ones of honour. I had earned every one of them.

There was one more blow to come my way though. My position with Sovereign was not as secure as I thought when I joined the company. Corporations in the 90s went through massive changes and Sovereign was no exception. During the first five years I was with the company, I saw two mergers and the company was re-structured two or three times. Each time the executives changed along with the policies. I was one of the lucky ones and survived each round of layoffs.

My responsibilities had changed and my job had become stressful. The only thing that mattered to the company was the bottom line and I no longer enjoyed my work. I was also becoming aware that I no longer fit the corporate profile. I was too old, in my late 50s, and the company was looking for young, over-educated, inexperienced people to mold to their liking. I certainly didn't fit that description. Coincidentally, I suffered a neck injury around that time, aggravated by the 10s of 1000s of miles I drove on company business. The company took advantage of my injury and persuaded me to make use of the disability program until I was officially laid off three years later. A year before I could have collected a pension. Yet again, I saw my dream for a stable life and comfortable retirement being pulled out from under me.

At the time, I considered being laid off from Sovereign a blessing in disguise, and perhaps it was, but in retrospect, from a financial point of view, it was a disaster. However, it gave me the opportunity to survey my life, pick up the pieces, reassess my options and look seriously at what I wanted to be when I grew up.

Originally my chosen career had been to be a wife and mother and, when my marriage failed and I became a single mom, it forced me to look for work outside the home. I thought I had chosen my career options carefully, but they were based on the needs of my family at each moment. I needed flexible hours and enough money to feed, house and clothe the children. Looking to the future or considering my needs never entered the picture. I accepted whatever work came my way and would solve the problem of the day. Most often these positions were selling jobs and my introverted nature struggled with the competitive nature of the work. When I suspected my days were numbered with Sovereign, I decided to moonlight and try my hand in the travel business, selling cruise vacations. That was a fun job and, yes, I got to cruise a few times. The perks were great but I couldn't handle the cut-throat competitiveness. In my career, I had literally sold everything from soup to nuts. I hated selling and I wasn't very good at it. I had added many skills to my portfolio, but I never felt that I became an expert at anything.

At my age, most people would consider being laid off as an opportunity for early retirement. Unfortunately, without a pension, that was not possible for me. Instead of retiring, I was planning a new career. I now had the time and opportunity to choose a way of life right for me, both personally and professionally.

I wrote a questionnaire for myself. I selected six jobs I had either done or thought I might enjoy doing. I made two lists, one for 'pro' (positive features) and one for 'con' (negative features). I listed the features important to me, and included: flexible hours, making a difference, travel, meeting people, teaching, competitiveness, rigidity, being appreciated, level of stress and anything meaningful to me, both positive and negative.

The careers based on these features, and the results, gave me an indication of where to start. I then asked myself, 'If I could do anything I wanted to, what would it be?' Four related things were at the top of my list: teaching, planning and presenting seminars, speaking and writing. I focused on teaching and seminars.

Before I could move forward, I needed to acknowledge some emotional shortcomings and find a way to deal with them. Two more questions emerged: What reservations did I have about this work and how would I overcome them? And, what were the emotional barriers that would stop me from succeeding? These last two questions had to be answered honestly, and the issues dealt with. For example, one of my biggest barriers was lack of confidence. I needed to work on believing in myself and building my self-esteem. These discoveries led to one last question: What did I have to do to get there? I created a roadmap, detailing every step I had to take and always keeping an eye on the destination, always moving forward. How to get from here to there included everything from a contact phone number, signing up for a teaching course and figuring out how to boost my confidence.

My self-questionnaire worked well. I earned the Teaching of Adults Certificate (my first experience with on-line learning) and I became an accredited specialist and facilitator in personality styles, another fascinating subject. My life included teaching at the local school board in the Continuing Education Department, and planning and conducting workshops on personality styles.

They say all work and no play makes Jack a dull boy (or Jill a dull girl). Finding a different social life was more difficult. I enjoyed my girlfriends but we didn't do a lot and I had no interest in dating or playing the bar scene. I enjoyed classical music and live drama but only went when I could find someone to go with. There was no reason I shouldn't go on my own. I just never got around to it. I solved this problem by purchasing season tickets to the symphony and the local theatre. I joined a choir and did some volunteer work. These were all enjoyable activities that gave me an opportunity to meet like-minded people. Going out and doing things on my own took some getting used to but I needed to get over the fear. Eleanor Roosevelt once said, "You must do the thing that you fear the most." It was frightening at first to be so alone and, sometimes, I had to force myself to leave the house. I was getting to know myself and my circle of friends was expanding.

The transition from a single mother of five to a successful, contented woman living in harmony with her authentic self was ongoing. I was refurbishing the vacant building into a palace fit for a queen, but no longer the queen of denial. I had learned to eat healthier food and go to the gym twice a week. I stopped worrying and my body and mind were in good shape for a grandmother of nine. I was preparing for a very different 'happily ever after.' I could enjoy perhaps another 20 years and reap the benefits from all those hard times. I thought that I had arrived by accident, but on reflection it wasn't the case. I made many choices from gut feelings and instinct. Had I been more focused, questioned my motives and shared my thoughts and opinions with others, some decisions would have been easier and overall achieved better results. Despite the shortcomings and lack of planning, things turned out okay.

It took me a long time to appreciate what I had. During my younger years, I spent my time fantasizing about a fairy tale life. After I married, I tried to make it come true. It was time to end the fairy tale and move on.

I wasted a lot of energy punishing Rodney for my pain. I spent years being a martyr and wallowing in the 'poor me' syndrome, not daring to move on with my life. I wanted Rodney to see how he had destroyed my life and caused me so much pain. I couldn't let go. Hidden in the back of my mind was this belief that if I allowed myself to be successful, I could no longer blame him and if I didn't blame him, who would be responsible for all my unhappiness and shortcomings? Most of all, I wanted him to feel guilt and pain, my pain that he inflicted on me. I wanted to scream out to the world, "Look what this man did to me!" I had to keep on punishing him until the world knew the truth. Ironically, my mind had twisted things around so that I was punishing myself. Rodney was oblivious to my pain and any guilt he might have felt was long gone. He had remarried and moved on with his life, thousands of miles away. So how was I punishing him?

Dawn Brown describes this very well in her book *That Perception Thing!*

"... we believe that the only way we can be happy is to turn back time and to change the ending of the story. But changing the past is impossible, and so we replay the story over and over with others, hoping each time that we can come out ahead."

No matter how hard I tried, the end of my story with Rodney will never change. It was time to close the book on the fairy tale, free up that energy and channel it into my personal growth.

Most single moms, in fact most mothers, are so programmed to put the needs of their children first and their own needs a distant second that they rarely think about their own personal growth. After my children flew the nest, a large part of me went with them, leaving an empty shell. I filled that shell with friends and activities I enjoyed. It's essential for women to do that or the shell will eventually crumble. There is still a large portion of space inside taken up by family, but the family is different now. My children have spouses and their own children. My role changed from parenting children to parenting myself. I was no longer a single mom of five children, but a single woman who is part of a great family.

I was moving into a different stage of my life. Because of my age, a little past 60, the word retirement sprang to mind. I could not envision myself as retired in the traditional way. I had no pension or savings, so it was not practical. I moved past those early expectations and began to see my retirement years as a new stage of my life, one I would embrace with excitement and anticipation. I would have to continue working to support myself but I enjoyed my work, so it was more like play. I learned to value myself and live for me.

When Katharine Hepburn died at the age of 97, the announcer briefly described her life, saying "She experienced life on her own terms, not at the whim of others." Those words were profound and would be my motto as I planned the next stage of my life.

As I got older, I reflected on past years. Instead of looking back at the pain and hardship, I took great pride in the things I had accomplished. I celebrated the successes and learned from the not so successful. I deliberately chose not to use the word 'failure,' as I believed it was a word that should have been deleted from our vocabulary. Failure is success turned inside out, as we figure out how to turn failure around and turn failure into success.

17

The Loving Faces of Success

How do you measure success: wealth, achievement, winning or fame? In our modern world most of us measure success this way. 'She has so much money, she must be successful.' An athlete may view the ultimate success by winning gold at the Olympic Games, film stars by how famous they are or by how much money they command. Can success be defined without wealth, winning or fame? The answer is a resounding "yes."

Of course the athlete who has trained for five years and wins an Olympic medal is successful. The businessman who makes a million is successful and Tom Cruise is a successful film star. But most of us are not athletes, millionaires or film stars. Our society would have us believe that this is an acceptable measurement of success but it is an unrealistic perception and sets us up for instant failure. For years, I suffered from what I called, 'success envy.' Have you ever noticed that it always seems that your friend, acquaintance, brother or sister is luckier than you? They have their life in order, their children are brighter or better behaved, their business is doing better than yours. I work just as hard, have great ideas and my kids do their best. So why am I not as clever or successful as they are?

We look at success as a measurement, which it is not. A measurement is a yard, a metre, a quart or a litre. Success reflects accomplishment and can only be measured in terms of the satisfaction, pride and achievement felt by each of us in our own way. We assume other people are doing well, but that is our own perception. We accept that money, winning medals and fame means success even if it is unreasonable for us to reach that particular kind of success.

My success has nothing to do with money (unless you count being financially creative on a shoestring budget), or athletics (unless you reward running up and down stairs with loads of laundry), and my only claim to fame is being a chairperson of the PTA. My success or successes are the loving faces of my children. I had been blind to just how lucky I am to have such wonderful children and I realized that the most important and successful job I have ever done or would ever do was raise them. We are not a perfect family and, like most families, we have our fair share of skeletons in the closet. But as families go, we are darn good.

So what led me to this re-evaluation of success? Five appreciative, successful adult children showing their love on Mother's Day. I was sitting in a fancy Italian restaurant, with Nathan and his family, enjoying an appetizer, a delicious strawberry salad. I was thinking about the events of the wonderful day drawing to a close. Nathan had brought not just his family but his old friend Dave who now lived on the East Coast and happened to be in town on business. Dave was one of the boys from Blackburn Hamlet who had spent much of his youth in our basement and he still thought of me as his second mom. I always thought I was just another meal ticket—teenage boys eat constantly—but Dave really thought of me as 'mom.' We reminisced over the old days. They enjoyed teasing me by letting slip a few of their antics that they thought I didn't know about. But it was interesting to hear their version of some teenage stories. The story of the time they nearly blew up the house trying to make fireworks in my basement was one I didn't need to know about! Probably a good thing I didn't know at the time. It was rewarding to know that my parenting had made a positive impact on their lives.

Katrina and I met at the local coffee shop to celebrate. She never ceases telling me how much she loves and cares for me. We have the most fabulous relationship and as we grow even closer, we are discovering how many interests we share. We had to work hard to have the relationship we have now, but it is worth every tear drop.

The day started out with two phone calls, the first from Alex in London, England. He had just returned from spending a two-week vacation with me. What a wonderful time we had together! Alex has nothing to do with his father and has changed his name to my maiden name, saying "I never knew my dad. You raised me and I want to carry your name." I think that says it all!

James phoned a little later that morning from Toronto. He is a sensitive man who is never shy to tell me how much he cares for me and appreciates the sacrifices I made over the years. We can talk for hours. It is special to talk and have so much in common with an adult son. After a great conversation, it was time for me to get ready to meet William and his family for brunch. Brunch was buffet style with copious amounts of terrific food and what seemed like a million choices. The highlight of the brunch happened as we were leaving. William handed me some flowers and a card. I started to open the card and he asked me to wait until I was home to open it. His wife, Linda, teased him saying, "Is it one of those mushy cards?" It was one of the most meaningful cards I have ever received.

The card read as follows:

Mom, I see how you live.
I see how you love.

The bar has been set pretty high.
I'm trying to be the best man I can,
when I'm not just trying to get by.
So maybe one day we'll both be amazed,
and we won't know how or just why,
but we'll see your example reflected in me.
If so, I'll have learned how to fly.

Single moms, wherever you are, whoever you are, believe me when I say, "It is all worthwhile." I am blessed. I am the luckiest, most successful woman in the world.

The love, appreciation and support saved me and re-energized my life. As I look back, I could have made different choices, I could have done some things differently. There is no doubt in my mind that had I taken the time to explore alternatives, I may have made my life easier. But at no time during those hard years did I ever imagine the rewards my grown-up children would bring to me.

At the end of this story it is my children, those same children who exhausted me emotionally, physically and financially, who give back to me. They fill my emotional being with their love caring and support. They help mend my physical body with their encouragement and advice to look after myself.

I picked up all those scattered pieces left by the tornado and I am whole again. With the help and support of my children, I have refurbished the rundown vacant building.

The children 'saved some for me.'

Please join us in the next chapter for a family dinner.

18

2003 - Join Us for a Family Dinner

Festive family dinners mark the times we usually get together—Christmas, Easter and Thanksgiving. It is rare when we can all be there at the same time but occasionally at Christmas we meet with only one or two family members missing. This is a time when we can catch up with the events in everyone's lives. I will take you to one of our family dinners so you can catch up with each of us in 2003.

Our traditional Christmas dinner is turkey with all the trimmings, recipes that have been handed down through four generations. How many people plan to attend dictated who hosts the dinner. A full house is 19 plus the dog, Trixie, who is now 18 years old and still going strong.

Nathan is the eldest, number one son, and he always carves the turkey. Nathan is a very successful film editor and producer. He owns his own editing business and two years ago was nominated for a Gemini Award for one of his productions. Nathan has an 11-year-old son, who is already taller than I am and is a computer whiz. Pouring the wine is William, number two son. William is a mechanical engineer for a large consulting firm. Last year, he was made an associate in the firm. His wife Linda is a part-time financial adviser and full-time mom to their three little boys. Nicholas is a shy little five-year-old. Christopher, age two, has a smile that would melt a stone, and baby Harrison is an adorable six-month-old. They have a beautiful new home in a suburban area on the other side of the city. As they have the largest house in the family, when everyone or almost everyone makes it for the family dinner, we gather at their home.

Katrina helps me in the kitchen. The men do their fair share, remember I raised them. Katrina is an administrative assistant, managing seminars and workshops. Her husband, Peter, works part time so he can be home with the children. He is a very brave stay at home dad. Julien is seven and a busy, mischievous little boy. Karoline just turned nine and she is as free spirited as her mother was at that age, a charming little princess. I tease Katrina as I point out the similarities in their personalities and she frowns as she imagines what might be in store for her as Karoline grows up. They live in the other side of the city and have the largest garden so, in the summer, we gather there for the annual family picnic. Katrina and I spend a lot of time on the phone. She is my confidante, friend and soul mate.

James, number four son and the baby of the family, is home for the holidays. He lives in Toronto. A very talented jazz musician, James plays the double bass. A free spirit like his sister, he plays in local bands and recently joined an orchestra. He recently returned to his day job teaching web design, after taking parental leave to look after his baby daughter while her mom, Dawn, worked on a Masters Degree. Annabelle is almost two and is tall just like her daddy. Alex, number three son, phones us from Italy. He is an executive chef who, until recently, worked in some of the best five star hotels in London, England. Alex and his Italian girlfriend Laura just invested in Laura's family's business, a small prestigious hotel on the south coast of Italy overlooking the Mediterranean Sea. I am eager to visit.

My mom is with us for her traditional Christmas visit. Mom still lives in England and is 83 years young going on 60. We are often taken for sisters and she is delighted. I am not so flattered, but very proud of her. Mom always brings a sense of propriety and dignity to the family as we brush up our table manners and wear our Sunday best clothes.

My career took another little turn. I am now a published author and am working hard on a speaking career. I took a part-time job at the local wine store, which is one of the most fun jobs I have ever had, and it helps to pay the bills. Finances are still a challenge and there is no man in my life. My circle of friends grows each day and I have some wonderful new friends and precious old ones. Martha and I lost touch and I haven't seen her in years but Carol and I have been friends for 32 years. We still spend hours talking and figuring out what the future holds for us.

Dinner is ready and there are 17 of us sitting at the table. This year we all squeezed into my house. Only Alex and Laura are missing this time. The dishes clatter and the conversation gets very loud. Heaping plates of turkey with stuffing, cranberry sauce and an English delicacy of bread sauce are passed around before the bowls of potatoes and vegetables. The gravy comes in a large, old Pyrex jug, which is fondly known as the 'family heirloom.' It has been around for years. It is scratched and ugly, but became part of the family dinner scene about 15 years ago because it was the only jug that would hold enough gravy for all of us. Now it is a symbol of our union as a family.

We remember the family stories about Eric the fluffy orange cat, Mom tripping over the tennis the ball and many others. We never tire of them and we always laugh until tears roll down our faces. Sometimes there is a little altercation between siblings but it quickly blows over. Some years there is a new story to be added or just a new version of an old story. The 25 pound turkey is diminished to a few leftover pieces and everyone finds room for a little piece of flaming Christmas pudding. The wine has been drunk and we loosen our waistbands as we relax and chat quietly over coffee. The children are getting restless. They are tired and overexcited so, before they demolish Grandma's house, it is time to leave. The day passed quickly. We hug goodbye and they take the little ones home to bed.

The family dinner is a cameo of my success, five grown children and seven grandchildren, (two more come later). What more could anyone ask for?

Perhaps, I might be ready for a little career success.

God just opened another window for me. I am embarking on another career and it's not retirement!

19

Fast Forward Eighteen Years - 2019

When I started this project I intended to re-write *Save Some for Me* and add a chapter or two to bring you up to date with my life as it is today. I read through the book with fresh eyes and changed my mind, making only minor revisions. I use the word minor deliberately because I chose to leave 90% of the writing alone. My writing style has changed over the years, as you will see in these final chapters. Some of my opinions and life perceptions have also changed so you may find some discrepancies. However, I felt it was important to leave much of the original wording intact as the discrepancies have more to do with a maturing and changing life styles than differences of opinion.

I debated long and hard about adding these chapters because *Save Some for Me* is a memoir of my life as a young wife, mother and empty nester. It is my story of overcoming spousal abuse, divorce and single motherhood and how I survived, which is amazing even to me. But survive I did. I moved on to a new and productive life inspired by the writing and publication of this book and I concluded that the choices I made since the tornado subsided were of value and contributed to the life I have now.

I ended Chapters 17 and 18 as a tribute to my success. My first success being the loving faces of my children. These final chapters are all about my second success as an author.

First I will bring you up to date. It goes without saying that not only have my children grown up, my eldest kids are not much younger than I was in 2003, and shockingly, I now have grown up grandchildren. The eldest is twenty-seven and youngest twelve. I admit that puts me within spitting distance of eighty. I do have a couple of more years but it's closer than I would like. If you are wondering whether I have any great-grandchildren, I'm happy to say no, not yet. It surprises even me to say that, as I love babies (perhaps the reason I had five kids). I know it will be a happy occasion when it happens but I'm not ready to add 'great' to Granny.

I have moved a couple of times since 2003 and now live in a condo apartment in the west end of the city, overlooking the Ottawa River, a place I love and hope to stay. The family has had their fair share of tragedy, spousal breakups, new additions and achievements, which is to be expected in a family of 21: five adult kids with spouses, nine grandkids, my mum and me. There are too many events to go into detail, so I will be brief.

My eldest son, Nathan has moved into my condo building with his adult son, no partner but a lovely girlfriend. My daughter, Katrina, is still with Peter. One child has flown the nest but the other yet to fly. My middle son, William and his wife Linda still live in the same suburban house. Their boys are grown and one has already flown the nest while one is almost ready to go and youngest finishes school. I am lucky that these three families live close by in Ottawa. The youngest boys chose foreign lands. Second youngest son, Alex, was living and working in Italy in 2003, but now lives with his wife and their two sons, my youngest grandsons, still in school, in the UK. My youngest son, James, has had a turbulent life, with an estranged girlfriend and young daughter. But finally things worked out and he escaped the cold Canadian winters and settled in warm sunny Costa Rica where he married Daniela. His daughter, my youngest granddaughter, finishes school this year.

When I wrote the first edition, my mom, who lives in the UK was 83. She is still with us and celebrated her 99th birthday a few days ago. My family has always included pets and the latest family addition is Miss Penny, an adorable Shih Tzu who turns two this year. She was preceded by Buddy Boy, a Bichon Frisé who succumbed to cancer and Trixie, who was 18 in 2003, died the following year. I still have fond memories of my old friends, some I still see. I lost touch with Martha a long time ago but I heard along the grapevine that she wasn't doing so good and her daughter had moved her to a retirement home in Toronto. Carol is still my best friend. She, like me, is still working and also, like me, has had many careers in her life. Our friendship is stronger than ever and, in May of this year, we celebrated 48 years of friendship.

Families scatter, lives and priorities change, and I am sad that we no longer have the family dinners. I miss them very, very much. I miss the siblings catching up, as they see little of each other on a daily basis, as well as the funny stories and teasing. But I am grateful that I have such wonderful memories.

Rodney died a few years ago and I am pleased that I made my peace with him. About a year before his death, I wrote him a letter, not of reprimand or anger, but of closure. I needed to shut the door on that part of my life, but I suspect it opened a new one for Rodney. He saw an opportunity. His second wife, Jean, was gone and I was still alive. I received phone calls and invites to visit. Memories of my visit to the cottage in Quebec surfaced as the offer of a first, or would it be a second refusal, was on the table. I had found closure and only felt sadness for this poor, unhappy man who had missed out on so much of life.

Much to my surprise, Rodney died an extremely wealthy man. I tried not to be angry but when I realized he had become wealthy while allowing his children to struggle in poverty, it was hard not to be upset (is there still some denial there—*upset* does not describe how I really felt). Rodney died suddenly and tragically alone. He had suffered terribly with ill health throughout his retirement. He left his estate to two of his children, you read it correctly, two, not five. Even in death, he tried to split the family and I suspect it was another attempt to hurt me. I'm happy to say it didn't work as the children shared his wealth with their siblings and helped me with my mortgage. No doubt he is turning in his grave!

I have mentioned before that retirement was not for me and I have achieved this great age without retiring and don't plan to anytime soon. I do take advantage of the retirement lifestyle. I don't dance to any other piper except my own. I go to bed when I need sleep and get up when rested. I haven't set an alarm clock for years. I choose my own schedule and have learned to say no when I don't have time or don't want to do something, although to be honest I'm still working on the last one. My finances are tight, raising five children alone leaves little for savings, so I am not able to travel. But, if I'm honest, travelling, particularly air travel, is such a hassle these days, staying close to home is not a hardship. I'm so lucky to live in a beautiful country like Canada. I don't need to travel.

Writing the memoir opened up a whole new meaningful career for me. I discovered I loved writing. I also wanted to pass my wisdom on to other women. After *Save Some for Me,* I began writing articles about spousal abuse and single parenthood. This led me to giving talks. Public speaking was not a task I enjoyed. In fact, my introverted personality objected strongly but I gave it a shot, hoping to help other women in similar circumstances. But my discomfort level was off the charts, so I scurried back to my writing desk.

Although public speaking was not for me, facilitating workshops and teaching adults suited me well. Having experienced difficulty learning as a child, but excelling in learning as an adult, I wondered why. I didn't hate school, in fact I enjoyed it. I also liked learning even though I didn't do well until I returned to learning as an adult. Facilitating workshops prompted me to go back to school a second and third time to get a diploma in teaching adults, studying learning styles and personality types.

During these courses, I realized that my difficulty in school was not with my intelligence, but how my brain processed information. I was incapable of giving snappy answers to the teacher's questions, which resulted in being falsely labeled 'a nice little girl but not very bright.' I am sure this had a major effect on my self-esteem, resulting in how I made choices, many of them not the wisest. I mention this last paragraph as an example to encourage anyone who struggled in school to give it another shot in adulthood.

Having spent thirty-plus years raising children, it was difficult to think of myself as anything but a mother. Even writing the memoir didn't seem real. I was on a constant search and tried many things. I became a Reiki Master, teacher, a counselor, mentor, facilitator and even a baker and entrepreneur. It is only on reflection that I realize how much each of these things contributes to my writing. But they were also a distraction, even procrastination. I suspect I had trouble believing in myself. Old messages messed with my confidence and there's always the fear of failure. How could I write if I wasn't very bright?

20

From Mother to Author

Even after I published *Save Some for Me,* I found it hard to believe I was any good and, as a result, I had difficulty promoting the book. But it gave me enough confidence to consider taking writing courses and I lucked out with an excellent instructor from the Institute For Writing in the USA. I registered for a course on writing articles and short stories. Anne Grant, my instructor, persuaded me to move to fiction. At the time, it seemed a big leap to go from writing about my life experiences to writing from imagination. Writing my life story had a downside as I felt exposed to the world. At least in fiction I could step away. Anne convinced me it really wasn't that different because writing fiction was nothing more than writing about experiences and putting them in a fictional setting. It sounded good to me so I tried it and discovered a new talent.

There is often someone in life that has so much faith in you that it rubs off and Anne was one of those people. One of Anne's parting comments made me feel like a writer, giving me the confidence to have faith in my own talent. I suspect it will stay with me for the rest of my writing life, although I do have to remind myself every now and again.

Anne Grant lecturer at IFW - Institute for Writers wrote...*"Susan, you have one of the strongest senses of 'story' I've run across in quite some time. You truly astonish me with the wealth and breadth of the stories you come up with. Treasure that part of yourself because it is a gift and no one can take it away from you and it cannot be bought. Moreover, I cannot teach it, but I know it when I see it."*

Anne's words flattered me extremely and, as much as I don't like to brag, I believe it's true. I had known for sometime that the story part of writing came to me easily. Anne's words gave me all the confidence I needed to pursue the craft.

It took several more years and many short stories before I ventured into novel writing. My first novel was a marathon that took me close to five years to write. In 2015, I published *The Blue Pendant*, which subsequently became a trilogy. Although Anne had retired from teaching, I let her know my first novel had been published and once again she boosted my confidence by announcing that I was now a novelist. I was a 'real writer,' validated by my mentor Anne Grant. I will release my eighth and possibly ninth book this year. Not bad for a third (or is it a fourth?) career.

My biggest regret is that I didn't start writing sooner, I found my calling at long last and answered the perpetual question 'What do you want to be when you grow up?' Perhaps I should rephrase that as 'What do I want to be after raising my family?' because that was always my chosen career. I just hadn't expected to do it alone, and never thought about what I would do when the family no longer needed me. In the traditional setting, my expectations were to retire with my husband. Ironically, had my fairy tale dream come true I would have retired. I would not have become a writer and I would never have found my passion. Sometimes being forced in to what seems to be the wrong direction, turns out to be the right one. There is always a silver lining within the darkest of clouds.

On reflection, there were hints of a hidden passion for writing. I have always been an avid reader. My childhood favourite authors where Enid Blyton, Arthur Ransom, The Brontë sisters, Jane Austen and Charles Dickens and, as I entered adulthood, the list grew and grew. I have a wall of bookshelves in my office full of books I've read with many more to read. Unfortunately, I struggled with the mechanics of English at school when writing essays or compositions as we called it and I always considered myself stupid. I was ashamed of being language challenged until one of my writing professors suggested that I was not the problem, but the way I had been taught. Speaking grammatically correct English was never a problem. All I needed was a good editor. Because of my difficulty, I was never encouraged to write. But I did write in secret and squirrelled away my journals, essays and short stories, which I'm sorry to say never saw the light of day and at some point, were thrown away.

Writing the novel is not the whole story. Once a book is written it has to be published. I quickly discovered that to publish in the traditional way required finding an agent and publisher, which would take several years. At my age anything can happen, as Maggie Smith said in *The Best Exotic Marigold Hotel,* " at my age I don't buy green bananas". So, I decided to self-publish—easy-peasy right? Well, not quite, self-publishing is a whole career in itself and a massive learning curve around technology. It would take too long to explain the whole process but briefly, the learning curve included, editing, cover design, formatting e-books, print books, uploading to retailers, advertising and marketing and don't let's forget social media. A large proportion I do myself others I delegate at my expense and ultimately I publish my books but it's time consuming, expensive and not very lucrative. However, I am proud to call myself an indie (independent) author and have full control over my books which traditionally published authors do not have.

I am a good writer, most days, and my books get good reviews and compliments from my fans. But my marketing skills are not great and, even if my books are good or even outstanding—that might be pushing it, sustaining sales is difficult. Even with five star reviews on Amazon, it will be a while before I make a living with my books. I sure hope I live long enough to see that day.

I originally wrote *Save Some for Me* to help women, especially abused and abandoned ones. Today, women have more options than I had or was aware of, safe houses and community support and the ability to speak out. But it wasn't always like that. Spousal abuse was brushed under the carpet and women were afraid to talk about it. A trip on the stairs or walking into a door explained the bruises. Excessive drinking was excused as a good time and verbal abuse was laughed off as teasing. Any woman who has suffered under the hands of a controlling man knows what I'm talking about. Those scars never completely go away, but there are lessons to learn. If I had my time over again, I would speak out right at the very beginning and make it clear that abusive and unkind behaviour was not acceptable. Although times have changed, I am sad to say I still see young women making excuses for abusive partners. My message is "DON'T." Be brave, speak up and ask for help.

People often ask me, "how did you do it?" and my reply is nearly always "I don't know, but you do what you have to do." In retrospect, I think the one thing I would do differently is put my needs into the equation as well as the children's welfare and I would make plans for my future. If you put time into perspective, I spent thirty-plus years raising five kids and, twenty-five years later, I am only just discovering my needs. Imagine how much more I could achieve both financially and career wise, had I planned my life after the children. I'm not complaining because I did okay. And that would be my second message to mothers, single or in a relationship, chances are you will have thirty to fifty years to do whatever you want. Don't waste that time, plan for it and enjoy it.

I hope I don't sound as if I'm bragging because that really isn't my style.

I have learned to acknowledge my accomplishments, which as I look back, are many. When I think of me as the shy, innocent, compliant, even fearful, twenty-year-old woman and the woman I am now, fifty-eight years later, I shake my head in disbelief that I survived, let alone thrived. I somehow muddled through the tornado of a broken marriage and single motherhood, picked up the pieces and struggled through career changes and, eventually, literally landed on the written page as a novelist.

I am not one for regrets or looking back. The past cannot be changed and opportunities lie in the future. But I sometimes ask myself if the end result would have been different if I had planned instead of muddling through. Perhaps!

Well, that's all the wisdom I have for today. Another fiction story is calling me.

The loving faces of success in my children 'saved some for me' in the first half of my adult life and capturing loving engaging words in my books to share with my readers 'saved some for me' in the second part of my adult life. I wonder, will there be a third?

Judi Dench's quote from *The Second Best Marigold Hotel*
"How many new lives can you have?... As many as you like."

A Final Quote

Your success and happiness lies in you. Resolve to keep happy, and your joy and you, shall form an invincible host against difficulties.

-Helen Keller-

Acknowledgements

My thanks for the second edition of *Save Some for Me* are a little complicated as this version of the book would never have happened if the first edition had not been published, stating the obvious.

In the beginning, Serena Williamson Andrew, a.k.a. Dr. Sharon Letovsky, my writing coach and mentor inspired me to write the book and guided me through the publishing process. Laurel Simmons, also my coach at that time, gave me the confidence to believe in myself. Psst! That was close to sixteen years ago. My heartfelt thanks to both of you for helping me start my writing career.

My family encouraged me and many friends supported me. A special mention to Kathleen and her late husband, Bob Bigras who, in spite of Bob's poor health, found time to cheer me on way back in 2003. Bob managed a glimpse of the galley copy but sadly, died before the official launch. Kathleen remains a close friend and great supporter of my work. To Cathy Burton, who was at my side long before I wrote the book, thanks a million.

I would like to name everyone who was involved, but the list is extremely long. During the months leading up to the publication of the first edition, my life went through many transitions that involved some wonderful people. Thank you to everyone.

When I decided to write the second edition, I had encouragement from previous readers and colleagues but it was mostly because of technology changes. At first printing there was no print-on-demand, electronic or audio books. I felt it necessary to bring *Save Some for Me* into the 21st century with an e-book as well as paperback. Audio will come later.

As always, many thanks and much gratitude to my writing groups, TOSS (The Ottawa Story Spinners) and the Ladies Historical Writing Group, whose feedback and comments continue to be invaluable.

The redesign of the cover was a challenge, a total of twelve people were involved in that decision, thank you everyone. A special thank you to Debbie Stenson and Nancy Morris who challenged me with unusual thought provoking questions, resulting in a new idea. The consultations concluded in this amazing cover designed by Rebecca of Rebecca Covers.

Editing this book was an especially tough job as I wanted the editing to maintain the original style of writing. Many thanks to my amazing editor, Meghan Negrijn, for a great job

About the Author

Susan A. Jennings was born in Britain of a Canadian mother and British father. She grew up in Nottingham, attended college in Sheffield and married a medical doctor. The family immigrated to Canada with three children (two more were born in Canada). Divorce changed her career path from wife, homemaker and stay-at-home-mom to single mom raising five children alone. Susan led an eclectic career to support the children, mostly in sales, selling, literary everything form soup to nuts. After her children flew the nest and many make-do careers, Susan eventually wrote a memoir. The memoir was the catalyst that set her off on her current writing career as a novelist. Susan frequently features both heritages in her stories. She writes historical fiction, particularly the Edwardian era and wholesome contemporary romance. She has raised five children, all grown up with their own families and has nine grandchildren. Susan lives and writes overlooking the Ottawa River in Ottawa Canada. The author of nine books including *The Sackville Hotel Trilogy, The Sophie Series, The Lavender Cottage Series,* several anthologies and many short stories.

You can connect with me on:

- http://susanajennings.com
- http://sajauthor
- http://facebook.com/susanajenningsauthor

Subscribe to my newsletter:

- http://eepurl.com/bgY6kb

Also by Susan A. Jennings

This book, *Save Some For Me* a memoir is her only nonfiction publication. Susan's fiction books include The Sackville Hotel Trilogy and The Sophie Series, both are historical fiction, from the Edwardian era to the cold war. She also writes wholesome, contemporary romance in The Lavender Cottage Series.

The Sackville Hotel Trilogy
is filled with romance, modern history, intrigue and even murder. An epic saga from Edwardian Britain through to the Cold war of the 60s.

The Blue Pendant - Book 1
Anna's Legacy - Book 2
Sarah's Choice - Book 3
Box Set - Books 1, 2, 3. E-book only
Check website for links http://susanajennings.com

The Sophie Series
A captivating historical WW1 series of love and loss. Heartbroken Sophie enrolls as a probationary nurse in 1915 London. She never imagines that nursing bombed out Londoners and battle-weary soldiers would trigger her own fears from a tragic past.

Prelude to Sophie's War - Book 1 and coming soon
Heart of Sophie's War - Book 2 Due for release in 2020
Check website for links
http://susanajennings.com

Ruins in Silk - A Duo Prequel

Her mother's death is the first of many unimaginable tragedies.

The prequel to *The Blue Pendant,* where this privileged young woman finds herself working as a maid at the Sackville Hotel and the prequel to *Prelude to Sophie's War* when she leaves the hotel to become a nurse in 1915 London. **Free download from my website** http://susanajennings.com

The Lavender Cottage Series

Out of heartbreak comes love the second time around. Katie is grateful for a fresh start as she moves into Lavender Cottage and meets the kind, handsome Piers Bannister, owner of the narrowboat 'Tranquil Days'. Katie is attracted to Piers as he is to her but…

When Love Ends Romance Begins - Book 1

Christmas at Lavender Cottage - Book 2

Truth and Lies - Coming soon - Book 3

Check for links http://susanajennings.com

Save Some For Me

And what about You? Could you survive an abusive man and raise five children, alone?

A heartrending story of one woman's struggle to survive spousal abuse and, consequently, single parenthood. It is the story of undying determination to succeed and the courage to see her life culminate as the fairy tale, happily-ever-after of her childhood dreams. It has a happy ending, really; but in a different perspective.

—Emily-Jane Hills Orford, award-winning author.

Check for links http://susanajennings.com

www.ingramcontent.com/pod-product-compliance
Ingram Content Group UK Ltd.
Pitfield, Milton Keynes, MK11 3LW, UK
UKHW041823200726
13854UKWH00002BA/514

9 781989 553039